ENDLESS PATH

Buddhism

This is a **FLAME TREE** book
First published in 2006

Publisher and Creative Director: Nick Wells
Designer: Lucy Robins
Project Editor: Sarah Goulding
Picture Researcher: Polly Willis
Production: Kelly Fenlon, Chris Herbert and Claire Walker

FLAME TREE PUBLISHING
Crabtree Hall, Crabtree Lane
Fulham, London SW6 6TY
United Kingdom
www.flametreepublishing.com

10
3 5 7 9 10 8 6 4 2

Flame Tree is part of The Foundry Creative Media Company Limited
Copyright © The Foundry 2006

A copy of the CIP data for this book is available from the British Library.

ISBN: 978-1-84451-518-9

Every effort has been made to contact copyright holders. In the event of an oversight
the publishers would be glad to rectify any omissions in future editions of this book.

Printed in China

Buddhism

Authors: Diane and Jon Sutherland   Foreword: John Bowman

**FLAME TREE
PUBLISHING**

Contents

Foreword

There were many Buddhas before Shakyamuni Buddha, the Sage of the Shakyas, 'the awakened one'. What distinguishes Gautama Siddhartha from his predecessors is that he was the founder of the spiritual path known as Buddhism. Buddhism is, however, more than just a spiritual path: it is a great religion. What distinguishes Buddhism from most other religions is that it is non-theistic. This means it is a religion that does not recognise the need for a supreme and pre-eminent creator god omniscient, omnipotent, all loving, omnipresent, self-existing, as distinct from humankind. It does not deny these qualities or attributes, though, but does not insist on them being bound to a particular being through a particular revelation designated to a specific time and place.

The Buddha was clear when it came to the discussion of matters such as the origin of the world, the cosmos and all the questions that appeal to people's natural curiosity and interest because they were speculative and not conducive to liberation. Buddhism is not opposed to questioning these matters, as was the case with the Christian church fathers and Galileo. There is no orthodox view as to the creation, how it came about, when it came about or if it took a week, 13.7 billion years or 14.7 billion years; there is no doctrinal view expressed either of who created the universe, 'how many angels can dance on a pin': all these matters are seen as diversions away from the central issue of why we suffer and what we need to do to suffer less. This view is particularly pertinent today, in an era of psychodynamic psychotherapy where we look for the causes of suffering in our past, the discovery of which is said to be the prize of the 'wooden spoon' because understanding alone is never enough to remove suffering.

The analogy given by the Buddha was that of a man who had been shot with a poison-tipped arrow which was still embedded in his flesh. Should he now stop to reflect on the origin of that arrow: where the wood was from; what tree and what branches; what feathers had been used in its construction; who had made it? Should he consider where the poison was from, who had shot the arrow, what was his family and to which clan did he belong? What should be done with this arrow? The Buddha said that he should not think about these things, but should remove the arrow as quickly as possible to prevent the poison from flowing through his system and killing him. This removal of the arrow is the substance of the teaching of the Buddha.

'Suffering I teach and the way out of suffering,' said the Buddha, and it is the recognition of necessary suffering that points towards the solution to suffering. The Buddha is often thought of as the great physician and therefore he needs to know the symptoms before prescribing the treatment. The Four Noble Truths are the condition and the Noble Eightfold Path is the treatment.

This is a practical way, not an intellectual exercise, and starts with good behaviour. Once we have learned to live a more or less decent human life and applied ourselves to the universal standards of decent behaviour (not killing or stealing, etc), we can then begin to cultivate and gentle the inner savage. Noble he may be but he has not yet been gentled, and the way of the Buddha is the gentling and transformation of the hot passionate heart of man, rather like the refining of gold that requires many stages before the pure metal gleams and sparkles. The gold has always been there but has been invisible to the eye because of the impurities to which it has been attached.

This refining process is the stuff of practice. Man has enormous potential for good or bad: now more than ever is a time for us to wake up and take full responsibility for our actions, on this little planet in a remote solar system on the edge of one of the smaller galaxies. If we fail to do so our future is limited. If we do there is no knowing the wonders that will be produced.

Will the planet survive us, will we survive? That entirely depends upon us and our actions. On a personal level we have to ask ourselves is happiness the accumulation of even more things: cars; houses; degrees; children; or is there another way? This other way is the way the Buddha discovered for himself so many centuries ago, and this way has been kept open by the generations of those who have followed in the Buddha's footsteps. It is open for us, too, should we wish to take that first step.

John Bowman, 2006

Origins and History

Buddha's Birth

It is difficult to unravel the historical Buddha from the legend. Buddha was born Siddhartha Gautama in Lumbini, near the present-day Nepalese-Indian border in about 563 BC. His father, King Suddhodana and mother, Queen Mayadevi, ruled the Sakya tribe. His name, Siddhartha, literally means 'one who obtains success and prosperity'. Before his birth it was believed he would either become an all-conquering monarch or a Buddha.

The wisest seer, a man called Asita, predicted he would become a Buddha, one who has supreme knowledge, much to the disgust of Gautama's father. His mother died seven days after he was born.

The Early Years

Until he was seven years old, his aunt Mahaprajapati raised Gautama
in one of his father's palaces at Kapilavastu, thought to be in present
day Southern Nepal or Bihar state of India. At a very young age he
had his first spiritual experience, when during a ploughing ceremony
while sitting under a rose-apple tree he effortlessly entered – without
trying – the first *jhana*, or meditative absorption.

As a child he was brought up in considerable luxury and security.
His father thought that if his son did not experience pain then
there would be no reason for him to turn to religion in later life.

He honed his athletic and technical skills, learning
to become a warrior and a proficient archer.

Marriage and Fatherhood

When Gautama was 16 he married his beautiful cousin, Princess Yasodhara. For the next 13 years they lived their lives in the royal court of King Suddhodana. The king built the couple three palaces, one for each season and continued to protect Gautama from any troubles or worries. The couple had a son when they were in their late twenties.

The Four Sights

Gautama was still not satisfied with his life. He had an inherent enquiring and contemplative nature. He made four excursions to a nearby town, which would change his life forever. On the first visit he met an old man. On the second he met a diseased man. On the third he encountered a body on its way to cremation. On his fourth visit he met a Holy Man who helped Gautama to realise that old-age, sickness and death signify suffereing and impermenance, and that people have little control over their own lives. The fourth sight gave him inspiration to change his life.

The Renunciation

On the night of his 29th birthday, Gautama decided to give up his life as a wealthy prince and leave the royal court without explanation. He abandoned his silk robes and adopted a simple robe, of a holy man. He cut off his long hair and set off in search of the truth, with only an alms bowl.

Gautama had become the Bodhisattva, or future Buddha, a penniless and homeless man, leading a life of self-mortification and spiritual study. His disciples abandoned him when they thought he had taken to a life of luxurious ease when he accepted rice gruel and washed when near to death.

The Great Enlightenment

Having given up his wife, family, kingdom and his disciples, he was completely alone. Gautama was determined to unravel the truth or die in the attempt. He spent seven weeks sitting under a Bodhi tree in Bodh-Gaya, in the present state of Bihar in India.

He slipped into deep meditation. He saw his past lives, how karma worked, how to overcome desire, attachment to existence and the clinging on to false views. He was visited by the demon, Mara, who tried to keep him in the world, tempting him with duty, sensual desire and then terror. Finally, on seeing the morning star, he became enlightened. He was no longer Gautama, but was now Buddha, the awakened one. He had found Nirvana, the extinction of greed, hate and delusion.

He realised that choices or conscious decisions had inevitable effects. Good action producing good results and bad action producing bad results.

'It is liberated, birth is exhausted,

the Holy Life has been lived out,

what was to be done has been done,

there is no more to come'.

Samyutta Nikaya

The First Sangha

After five or so years, Buddha delivered his first sermon in a deer park at Sarnath, Isipatana (near modern Benares, in India). This launched his 45-year teaching career.

Buddha was able to deliver the fundamentals of what would become Buddhism. Buddha had been reluctant to teach, but he had been persuaded by Brahma that many people would benefit from being exposed to his teaching.

Five disciples that had left him earlier now became the first five members of the Sangha, or Buddhist order. One of them instantly attained the status of Arhat, or the 'one with enlightened wisdom'.

Buddha's Teachings Until Death

Over a relatively short period of time Buddha established a reputation in Hindustan, by converting thousands of people to the Dhamma, or Buddhist teaching. It was during these early times that he delivered 'The Fire Sermon'.

He returned to his home and family in 527 BC and converted most of his tribe. Four years later his father died and Buddha ordained his aunt, the first woman to be ordained. From then on women were admitted to the Sangha.

He travelled around northern India, attracting many thousands of people: beggars, barbers, merchants, princes and kings, men and women, even murderers. There were several attempts on his life.

The Bodhi Tree

The place where the Buddha was enlightened is now a sacred site and pilgrimage centre visited by pilgrims throughout the ages. The Mahabodhi temple is here, where there is a tree that is said to be descended from the one under which the Buddha was enlightened.

Parinirvana

In 483 BC, aged 80, Buddha died, having achieved his goal of spreading his teaching to the greatest number of people. He died from food poisoning, in the company of his followers, in a forest near Kusinagara, Nepal. His last words were:

'Impermanent are all compounded things; strive on heedfully'.

Some Buddhists celebrate Nirvana Day, the Parinirvana, in February. It is an opportunity to think about their lives and how they can work towards the perfect peace of Nirvana. Nirvana is the ultimate aim and believed to be the end of rebirth. It is reached when all want and suffering has passed.

The Buddha's Footprints

The person of Buddha was
not represented in art, except
as symbols: the footprints,
the pillar of fire, the empty
throne, the wheel of the law
(dharmachakra) the stupa
(representing the death of
the Buddha), the Bodhi tree
and a pillar with a lion on top.

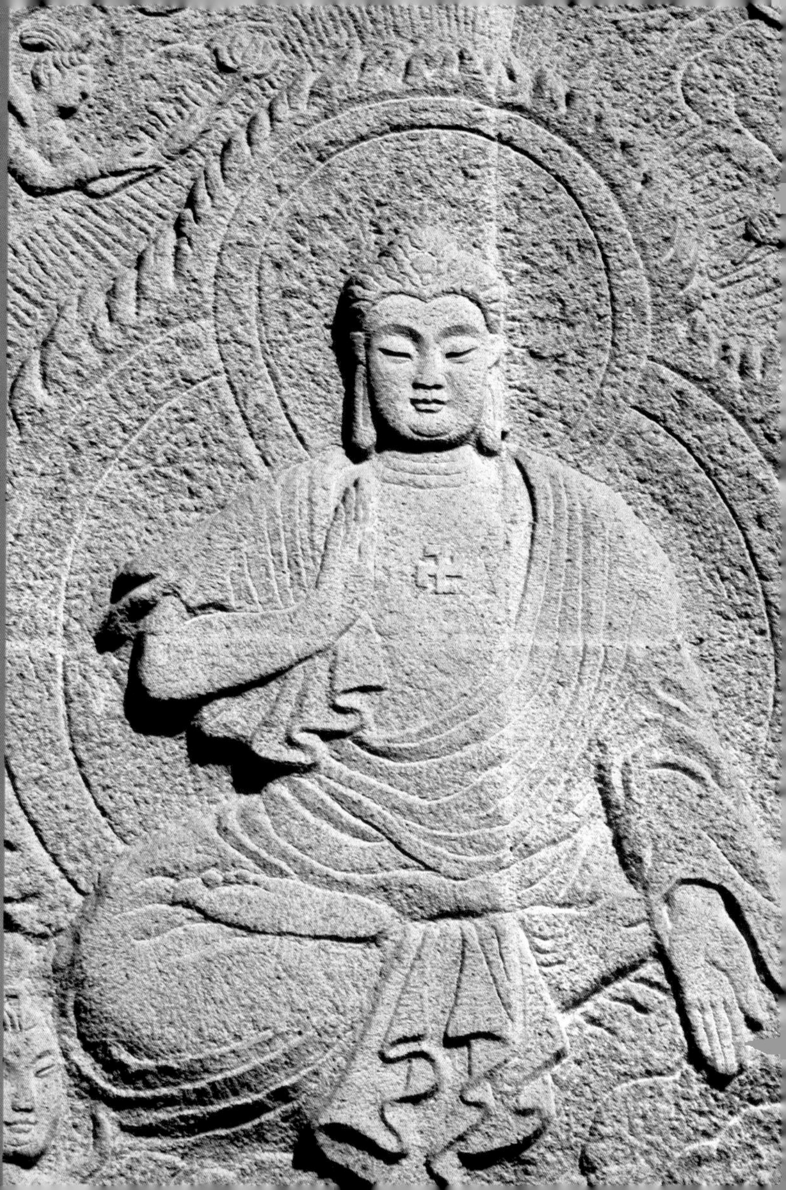

The Tipitaka

The Tipitaka, or teachings, are said to consist of three baskets: the Vinaya (rules of the monastic orders); the suttas or sutras (collections of sayings and sermons); and the higher philosophy and commentaries.

The Vinaya Pitaka

A monk called Upali collated the Vinaya Pitaka, or discipline basket, derived from Buddha's teachings. It is a set of 227 rules and regulations for the monastic community, or Sangha. There are additional rules for nuns. It gives guidance for the Sangha with their interactions with the community and with one another.

The Sutta Pitaka

The Sutta Pitaka, or discourse basket, focuses on Buddha's teachings on doctrine, behaviour and meditation techniques and was compiled by Ananda, Buddha's cousin.

The Abhidharma Pitaka

The Abhidharma Pitaka, also known as the higher knowledge or special teachings basket, was collated by Buddha's successor, Mahakashyapa. It contains songs, poetry and stories about the Buddha and his past life. It covers Buddha's philosophy and psychology. Part of it is the Dhammapada, which are sayings of Buddha, based on his daily life.

'The fickle, unsteady mind, so hard to guard,

so hard to control, the wise man straightens,

as the fletcher straightens the arrow'.

Verse 33, Cittavagga (The Mind), *Dhammapada*

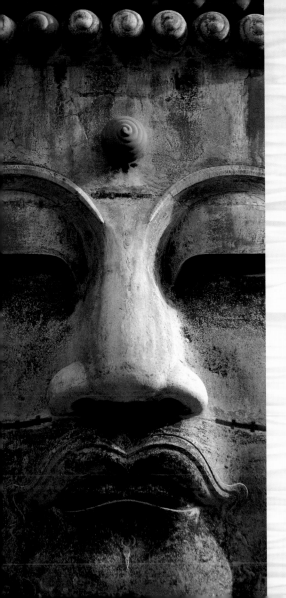

The Message of Buddhism

The Three Signs of Being

The three signs of being are in essence the three characteristics of all phenomena, or the ability to see things as they really are.

Change

Impermanence. Everything is always changing, whether physical, mental or emotional. Nothing stays the same so real stability is an illusion and even relative stability is at best a temporary state of balance. Our thoughts, moods and bodies are born, gain strength, then deteriorate and cease to be.

Suffering

Also known as dukkha, or unsatisfactoriness. These are feelings of insecurity and frustration that arise from attachment. As nothing lasts indefinitely many things are taken away from us before we can fully enjoy them. Individuals want security, satisfaction and happiness, but we are always trying to grasp it as it is just out of reach.

No-I

Buddha denied the soul. Furthermore, there is no permanent essence in anything, including ourselves. We spend much time and energy defending a non-existent I, Me or Mine. This is the central delusion in Buddhism, one that the Buddha saw through on his enlightenment.

The Message of Buddhism

'Suffering I teach and the

way out of suffering.'

The Buddha

The Four Noble Truths

The first noble truth is that suffering exists (dukkha). The second noble truth says that there is a cause for suffering, namely desire. The third says that suffering can be overcome by the vanquishing desire, and the fourth noble truth says that the way out of suffering is the Noble Eightfold Path.

The First Noble Truth: Life Means Suffering

Dukkha states that suffering is real, universal and has many causes. Human nature is not perfect and neither is the world in which we live. During our lives we will suffer sickness, injury, pain, tiredness, old-age and eventual death. We will suffer fear, frustration, depression, disappointment and sadness.

The world is subject to impermanence: in other words a person cannot permanently keep what they strive for and people and things will pass by and out of our grasp.

There are levels of suffering, but also positives, such as comfort, happiness and ease, but these too pass.

The Second Noble Truth: The Origin of Suffering is Craving

There is a cause for suffering, essentially the desire to possess and control things. Ignorance or lack of understanding of how our mind is attached to impermanent things causes craving and clinging. Desires may be sensual, the pursuit of fame or the desire to avoid unpleasant sensations.

All objects, whether physical or conceptual, are transient. Their loss is always inevitable and suffering will always follow their loss.

What we call 'self' is merely an imagined entity. We are all just a part of the ceaseless becoming of the universe. The idea of self is a delusion because there is no abiding self. It is the illusory self that clings, wants and has aversion.

The Third Noble Truth:
The Cessation of Suffering is Attainable

There is an end to unecessary suffering. It ceases when the individual achieves Nirvana. The mind experiences complete freedom, liberation and lack of attachment. Any desires or cravings are eliminated.

The individual must attain dispassion, extinguishing attachment and clinging. By achieving this suffering can be overcome. The attaining and the perfecting of dispassion is only a process of many levels on the path to Nirvana.

Nirvana is difficult to attain, as it is not comprehensible to those that have not yet attained it. Nirvana means freedom from I, Me and Mine, and freedom from worry, troubles, complexes, fabrications, ideas and opinions.

The Fourth Noble Truth: The Path to Cessation of Suffering

This is the path to the end of suffering, through gradual letting-go of the self and the cultivation of heart and mind. The Eightfold Path is the Middle Way, between excessive self-indulgence or hedonism and the extreme of self-mortification or asceticism. It eventually leads to Nirvana and the end of the cycle of becoming.

It is believed that the path to the end of suffering can take several lifetimes. Each rebirth is subject to the law of karma. Delusions, ignorance and the resulting aversion and craving will gradually fade as progress is made on the Eightfold Path.

The Noble Eightfold Path

The Noble Eightfold Path describes the way to end suffering, as described by Buddha. It comprises eight aspects of life, split into three connected categories. The first two are related to wisdom, the next three to ethical conduct and the final three to mental development.

Right Seeing or View

This is both the beginning and the end of the path. It means to see and to understand things as they really are and to understand the Four Noble Truths. This is an essential part of wisdom, requiring the individual to see and understand the imperfect impermanent and essence-less nature of objects and ideas.

Right Thoughts and Intentions

This is another aspect of wisdom. It means showing the commitment to ethical and mental self-improvement. The right intentions are the intention of renunciation, of goodwill and of harmlessness.

Buddha distinguished these three intentions to resist desire, anger and aversion and not to think or act cruelly, violently or aggressively.

Right Speech

This is the first that is concerned with our actions and their consequences. It means to speak appropriately as the situation demands, avoiding lying, criticism, condemnation, gossip or harsh language. Buddhists believe that words driven by the passions or fires of desire anger and delusion break or save lives, make enemies or friends, start wars or create peace. It means to speak without animosity or greed, to speak in a friendly, natural warm and gentle manner and not to waste words.

Right Action

Right Action suggests that the right conduct is free of enmity, aversion or blindness due to the passions obtained by following the Five Precepts. It suggests there is a right action, abstaining from harming sentient beings, abstaining from taking what is not given and abstaining from sexual misconduct. Unwholesome actions are said to lead to unsound states of mind.

Right Livelihood

This means that an individual should earn their living in a wholesome way and that wealth should only be gained legally and peacefully.

Buddhists believe that avoiding dealing in weapons, living beings, meat production and butchery, or the selling of intoxicants and poisons, including alcohol and drugs, is not conducive to happiness.

Right Effort

Right Effort is the first of the paths leading to mental development through concentration and meditation. This means the promotion of good thoughts and the conquering of evil thoughts. Misguided effort detracts the mind from its task, causing confusion. Right effort should prevent unwholesome states and maintain perfect wholesome states through self-discipline, honesty, benevolence and kindness.

Right Mindfulness

This involves becoming aware of your body, mind and feelings. Right Mindfulness or awareness needs clear and unclouded perception. It allows the individual to be aware of the processes that govern conceptualisation so that thoughts can be noticed and allowed to pass. Underpinning this are the four foundations of mindfulness/awareness: contemplation of the body, feelings, state of mind and phenomena and the path.

Right Contemplation

Right Contemplation or Concentration, requires the individual to achieve a higher degree of consciousness. Concentration is often described as one-pointedness of mind: 'being at one with' where an individual's mental abilities are unified and directed onto one particular object or problem. This concentration is developed through meditation, which allows focus.

'All that we are is the result of what we
have thought: it is founded on our
thoughts, it is made up of our thoughts.'

(Dhammapada, Chapter 1:1-2)

The Three Fires

After his awakening, the Buddha delivered a sermon to 1,000 fire-worshipping ascetics. He said the real fire is not outside; 'your house is on fire, and burns with the three fires; there is no dwelling in it'. By this, he meant the human body and the three fires that burn within it. He identified them as desire or wanting and craving, anger, and delusion. He called these energies fires because they are untamed and uncontrolled passions, they rage through the individual and hurt themselves and others. They can, however, be controlled by spiritual training and transformed into the warmth of humanity. It is said that 1,000 monks were released from their desires to follow a purer path.

'The fire of lust burns lustful mortals

Who are entangled in the sense-objects.

The fire of hate burns wrathful men

Who urged by hate slay living beings.

Delusion's fire burns foolish folk

Who cannot see the holy Dhamma.'

Itivuttaka, 93.

The Six Paramitas

The Mahayana emphasises the aspiration to become a Buddha, which is based on compassion for all beings. The first step in the path is to generate a Buddha heart, or Bodhichitta, which is the aspiration toward enlightenment, which arises from the inate potential for enlightenment. They should practice the six paramitas, or perfections.

Giving

Dana: this is the giving of material and non-material things, providing services of all kinds, helping others and teaching the Dharma. Giving of oneself to everything, wholeheartedly.

Moral Discipline

Also known as Sila, this means living according to the ethical rules or precepts and, at all times, restraining the senses and the passions. Not to harm, not to take that which is not given, not to misuse speech, to indulge in sensual misconduct, to avoid becoming intoxicated.

Patience

Also known as Kshanti, this is the means of overcoming anger, dealing with ill-will or hatred. At all times the individual should maintain inner peace and tranquillity.

Energy

Also known as Viriya, this requires the individual to abandon laziness and procrastination. Having done this, they should strive to be as energetic as possible in all ways, particularly in the practice of the teachings toward liberation.

Meditation

Also known as Dhyana, this revolves around developing and cultivating awareness. Along with awareness is the increase in concentration and insight into all matters.

Wisdom

Also known as Prajna, which means seeing the true nature of things. With it comes the realisation of emptiness (Sunyata) and the truth.

Buddhist Principles

The teachings of Buddha are not to do evil, to cultivate good and to purify the heart. Buddhists value loving kindness, patience, humanity and giving. Above all, they value compassion. Closely associated to this is harmlessness, in which the compassionate causes no harm to any other beings.

Buddhism places an emphasis on self-reliance derived from the Buddha's own life and teachings, that individuals should not believe anything merely because they have been told, until they have tested it for themselves. Buddhism aims to help people live their lives in a practical self-reliant and independent way.

The Precepts

The precepts are recommendations rather than commandments. The individual is encouraged to use their own intelligence and common sense to apply the rules. They are the essential guidelines for ethical conduct and are an integral part of the Eightfold Path.

The first five are mandatory for every Buddhist, although the fifth is often not followed to the letter. Precepts six to ten are directed towards those in monastic life. Ordained Theravada monks promise to observe no less than 227 precepts.

Explanation of the Precepts

The five basic precepts are to undertake the rule of training to:

1. Refrain from harming living beings
2. Refrain from taking that which is not freely given
3. Refrain from sexual and sensual misconduct
4. Refrain from wrong speech, including lying, idle chatter, malicious gossip or harsh speech
5. Refrain from becoming intoxicated by drink and drugs that lead to carelessness and self-harm.

The five precepts are also known as the five great gifts. They have not changed since the time of the Buddha.

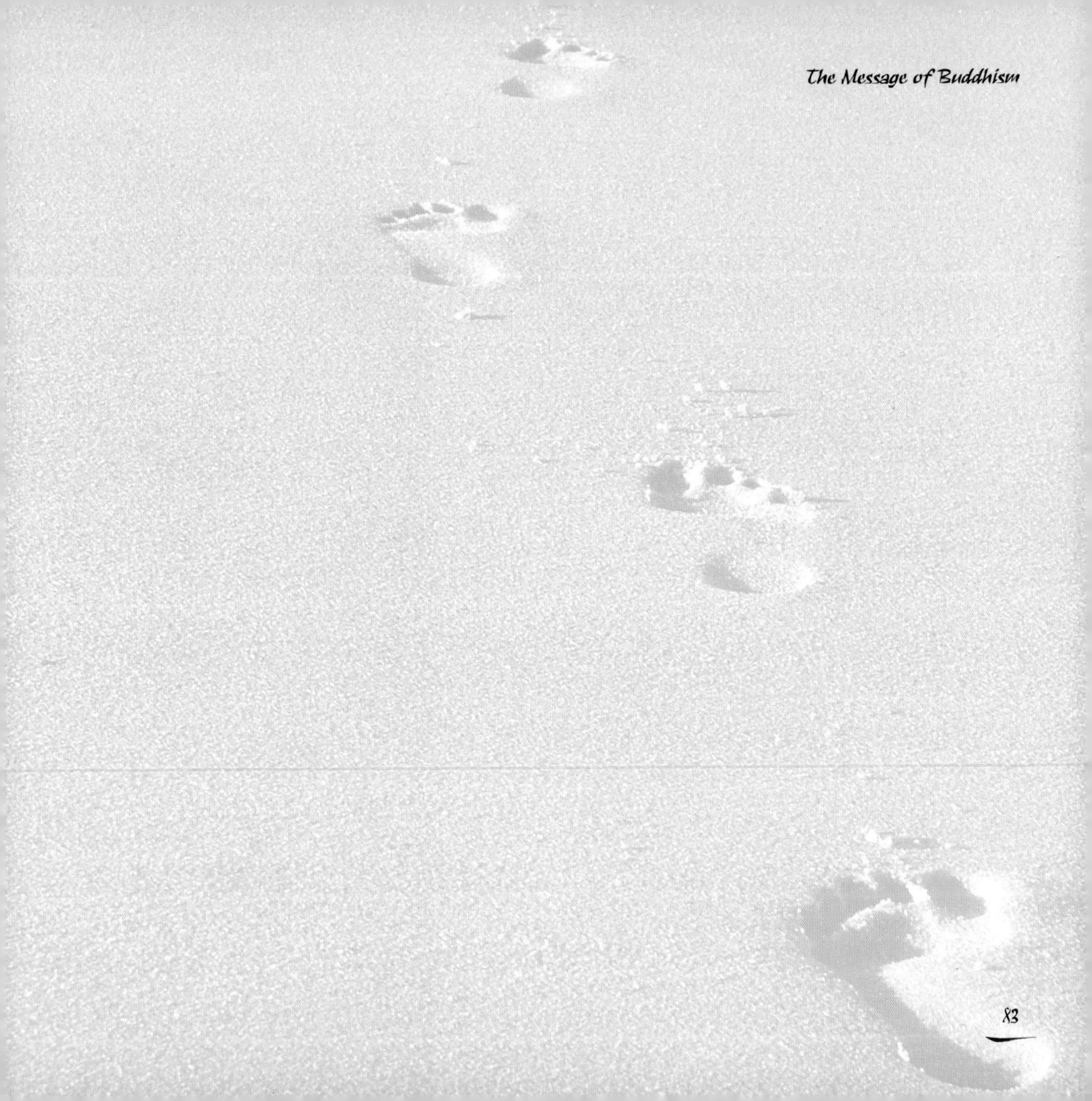

The Five Mindfulness Trainings

Some Tibetan Buddhists follow the five mindfulness trainings, which are adapted from the first five Buddhist precepts. They are the foundation ethics.

First Training

This first step begins with the recognition that suffering is caused by doing harm. The individual commits to cultivating compassion and to learn how to protect all beings. They determine to do as little harm as possible.

Second Training

The second step begins with recognising that suffering is caused by taking that which is not freely given; theft, oppression, social injustice and exploitation. The individuals commit themselves to sharing their time, energy and resources with those that are in need of their help. They undertake not to steal or possess anything that belongs to others.

Third Training

The third part recognises that great suffering is caused by sexual misconduct. The individual undertakes not to engage in sexual relationships that might cause suffering to self or others.

Fourth Training

The fourth training recognises that suffering is caused by unmindful speech and the inability to listen to others. The individual commits to speak truthfully, to inspire hope, joy and self-confidence. They further undertake not to spread gossip, use language that could cause division or family or community rifts and to help reconcile and resolve conflicts.

Fifth Training

This recognises that suffering is caused by greedy consumption. The individual undertakes to restrain from excess eating, drinking and general consumption, including watching television programmes, films, reading books and magazines. Fundamental to this is to follow the Middle Way. Careless and greedy consumption is believed to cause suffering, violence, fear, anger and confusion.

The Wheel of Life

The Wheel of Life is variously known as the Wheel of Dharma, Existence, Law, Rebirth, Samsara and Suffering. It is a six-spoke wheel, usually held by the jaws, hands or feet of a fearsome god, Yama, Lord of Death. The outer rim has 12 sections and the spokes divide the wheel to represent six worlds or realms of existence.

In each of the six realms there is always at least one Buddha depicted to help souls find their way to Nirvana.

The 12 links around the outside shows the law of karma, birth, old-age, sickness and death. It can be broken by abandoning attachment.

Core Beliefs

Buddhism, like many of the great religions of the world, is divided into a number of different traditions. Most of these traditions have a common set of fundamental beliefs.

Key fundamental beliefs are: the Four Noble Truths; the three fires of desire, anger and delusion; the three signs of being (suffering, impermanence and no-I) and the way out of suffering through understanding the law of action (or karma), which is that one's intentional actions lead to happiness or misery and the actions required to find liberation are delineated in the Middle Way and the Noble Eightfold Path.

The Buddhist Temple

Many Buddhists have a shrine in their own
homes, with a simple image of the Buddha,
candles and an incense burner. The temples
are often beautiful, but like the shrine are
symbolic representations of a Buddhist's
devotion to what they regard as being the
most important aspect of their lives. It is
forbidden to indulge in empty rituals.

Early Buddhism

The Spread of Buddhism

Buddhism spread southwards from Northern India to Sri Lanka, Myanmar, Indo-China, Thailand and other Southeast Asian countries. It also moved to the north and into the Himalayan region, as well as Tibet, Mongolia, Central Asia and then to China, Korea and Japan.

Buddhism was obliterated in India during the Islamic incursions of the 11th century AD. Communism almost eradicated Buddhism in China, Vietnam and Tibet, but there is now a strong resurgence. It is also attracting increasing numbers in Europe and the Americas.

Buddhism thrives in Sri Lanka, Myanmar, Thailand, Korea and Japan. Primarily, Theravada (southern), Mahayana (northern) and Vajrayana (Tibetan).

Pilgrimage

There are four key Buddhist pilgrimage sites located primarily in the Ganges Valley of India. Lumbini is where the Buddha was born. Bodhgaya is where the Buddha attained enlightenment. At Sarnath the Buddha proclaimed the first turning of the wheel of the law. Kushinagara is where the Buddha preached his last sermon and where he died.

Theravada School

This is the school of Buddhism in South Asian countries, including Myanmar, Cambodia, Thailand and Sri Lanka. It is based on the Pali Canon.

In the 3rd century BC, missionaries were sent to various countries by the emperor Ashoka. Mahinda and Sanghamitta taught throughout Sri Lanka. The sangha subsequently wrote down their teachings probably around 25 BC in the Pali language.

Theravada means 'the doctrine of the elders', the elders being the senior Buddhist monks. Buddha's teachings are seen as a guide: ways and instructions in which people can understand the truth; they are not held sacred in a fundamentalist manner nor are they considered to be divine revelation.

Mahayana School

In the first century BC, Sanskrit was used as the written language for the Buddhist schools in India. At this time there were new developments and further teachings. These developments helped produce the Mahayana, or 'great vehicle' teachings.

Mahayana is most strong in Tibet, Mongolia, China, Korea and Japan. The particular characteristic of this form of Buddhism is to emphasise the fact that each person can become a Buddha monk and layman alike, and work for the happiness and welfare of all. New texts simply reiterate this approach.

Mahayana Buddhism is a collection of Buddhist traditions, including Zen, Pure Land and Tibetan Buddhism.

Vajrayana School

This is considered to be the third wave of Buddhist development, which took place around AD 500. It is often known as Tantric Buddhism or the third turning of the wheel.

The principle example of this form of Buddhism is the one found in Tibet and in Japan, known as Shingon. Vajrayana Buddhism is fairly complicated, but colourful, and stresses the importance of a teacher or guide, often known as a 'guru', or in Tibetan a 'lama'. The teacher trains the temperament of the student and explains and passes on teachings.

They view the universe as consisting of energy and therefore try to transform and refine energy through yogic exercises, meditation, ceremony and chanting.

Buddhism in Tibet

The Indian Buddhist master, Atisha, reintroduced Buddhism to Tibet in the 11th century. He was asked to do so by the then-ruler of the Ngari region.

Atisha's presentation of the teachings is known as the Lamrim (stages of the path to enlightenment).

In the 13th century Tibetan Buddhism was further developed and promoted with the reforming of monasteries and emphasis on morale discipline and meditation. New commentaries were written for the sacred Buddhist texts.

Pure Land Buddhism

Pure Land Buddhism began in India in the 2nd century BC. It spread into China by the 2nd century AD and as far as Japan by the 6th century AD.

Japanese monks simplified the teachings and practices to enable most people to understand them, leading to a huge increase in popularity.

Pure Land Buddhism offers a way to enlightenment for those who cannot handle the subtleties of meditation or cope with long rituals. Followers chant the name of Amitabha Buddha in the hope that one will be reborn in the Pure Land, a stepping-stone towards enlightenment and liberation.

The Shin Sect

A century after the major development of the Pure Land Buddhism in the 12th century AD, a new disciple, Shinran, brought a new understanding. He taught that what was of most importance was faith, not necessarily the chanting. He believed that chanting on its own, without faith, had no value.

Shin followers believe that liberation is the consequence of a person achieving true faith in the Amitabha Buddha, coupled with their vow to save all beings that trust in him. Shin Buddhists believe that faith is a gift from Amitabha Buddha. A sinner with faith would be made welcome in the Pure Land.

Tibetan Buddhism

By the end of the 8th century AD, Buddhism was a major influence in Tibet. The Tibetan king invited two Buddhist masters to his country and had the Buddhist text translated into Tibetan.

Tibetan Buddhism has a number of rituals, spiritual practices and the use of mantras and yogic techniques. The supernatural is important, with gods and spirits taken from earlier Tibetan religions.

Tibetan Buddhism is strong in monastic communities and among the population, but it is a religion in exile. China has occupied Tibet since 1959. The spiritual leader, the Dalai Lama has lived in India ever since.

Zen Buddhism

Zen Buddhism is a school of Mahayana Buddhism practiced in Japan. Zen is derived from the Chinese word *ch'an*, which is the Chinese pronunciation of the Sanskrit word *dhayana*, which effectively means 'meditation'. Ch'an can be traced back to the 6th century AD. Most of the great Zen masters date back to between the 7th and 9th centuries AD.

Although its roots are in India, it has been influenced by Tao on its journey through China and Korea and into Japan. During the twentieth century it spread into the West.

Zen is an attempt to lead the full life without being misled by language or seemingly logical thought. Zen appears paradoxical but it is not. It requires intense discipline, which then results in spontaneity and freedom from the delusion of I.

'All beings by nature are Buddhas, as ice
by nature is water. Apart from water there
is no ice; apart from beings, no Buddhas.'

Hakuin Ekaku

korean Buddhism

Seon Buddhism is most significant in Korea, the largest sect being the Chogye Order, accounting for 90 per cent of Korean Buddhists.

Buddhism arrived in Korea in the 4th century AD and became the state religion by the 7th century. A Korean monk called Pomnang introduced Seon. By the 9th century it had become the dominant form of Buddhism in Korea. It is closely linked to Zen Buddhism as the Korean word for the Chinese *ch'an*, or Zen, is *Seon*.

Seon focuses on enlightenment by sudden awakening. But even when a person realises that they are innately Buddha, they continue to practice.

Nichiren Buddhism

Nichiren Buddhism began in medieval Japan. Many consider that Nichiren Daishonin was the Buddhist Martin Luther. He tried to reform Buddhism and Japanese society by his teachings, based on the Mahayana scripture, known as the Lotus Sutra.

Nichiren believed that he was living in a degraded age, where Buddhist teachings were misinterpreted and, as a consequence, bad things happened.

He believed that living beings could attain enlightenment through chanting and human revolution and this would be the only way to create a truly good world.

He believed rival Buddhists would go to Hell and was subsequently exiled twice. Many of his disciples were executed.

Common Features

The different traditions place varying emphasis on aspects of teaching and practices. Many of the fundamental parts go back to the Second Council, 100 years after the death of Buddha. The rules of monastic life and elements of the Dhamma are common to many of the schools' traditions.

The Three Jewels

The Triratna can be found on friezes, coins from the northern Punjab, Parthian coins and on Dharma wheels.

The Three Jewels symbol, or Triratna, was also found on a Buddha footprint in Gandhara. They are often known as 'the triple gem'. They represent a lotus flower within a circle, a diamond rod and a trident with three branches, which represent the three jewels of Buddhism: the Buddha, the Dharma and the Sangha.

The Three Jewels are seen as the manifestation of the teachings, the form they take and the practice, and they are seen as a guide, a protection and a refuge.

The Dharma

The Dharma is one of the Three Jewels. Many regard it as the ultimate and transcendent truth, beyond worldly things. The Dharma is also the universal law of nature inherent in all things. The laws of nature were not created by the Buddha, but merely rediscovered by him. Dharma can also refer not just to the sayings of the Buddha, but later interpretations and developments, which helped expand upon the teachings.

Others see the Dharma as a useful set of ideas and a code with which to live their lives.

However, many Buddhists regard the Dharma as simply meaning the teachings of the Buddha.

The Buddha

The Buddha is an essential part of the Three Jewels, the Buddha meaning the 'awakened one'. The Buddha is seen as the primary source of both authority and of inspiration. His life experiences illustrate to followers that there is a means of escaping from a world of suffering. Above all, this is achievable through their own efforts.

He is also revered in this respect as he illustrates the way to reach Nirvana and this adds to his status.

The Three Jewels are also known as the Three Refuges. In the insecurity of the world, they are seen as a place of protection and comfort.

'I go for refuge to the Buddha. I go for refuge to the Dharma. I go for refuge to the Sangha.'

Traditional Refuge Prayer

The Sangha

The Sangha is, in effect, a living example of the teachings of the Buddha. They are the community of monks or nuns that devote their lives to following the Buddha's teachings and, in this respect, they are an example to all, revered, as they follow the Buddhist path.

They are highly valued as they offer support, not only to one another, but also to the wider Buddhist community.

Members of the Sangha have some degree of training, and all are ordained monks or nuns, except novices. They are seen as providers of comfort and protection and are an integral part of the Three Jewels or Refuges.

In the Far East the Sangha is expanded to include all followers of the Buddha.

karma and Rebirth

The Wheel of Life is an ancient symbol, which illustrates the cycle of birth, life and death. When one complete revolution of the wheel is completed life begins again with rebirth.

Karma is a Sanskrit word that literally means 'action'. The concept of karma existed in India before the Buddha, but became an important part of Buddhist philosophy.

Buddhism suggests that individuals are responsible for their own happiness or suffering. These are dependent upon previous actions. Good action leads to happiness and bad action leads to future suffering for one's self and others.

Only actions that are deliberately intended will have moral or karmic consequnces.

The Law of karma

The Law of Karma connects actions with resulting forces. Karma means actions wholesome (*kusala*) or unwholesome (*akusala*). Acts have to be intentional to have karmic consequences. Harming or hurting someone accidentally is not considered to be morally wrong.

What we do now has an impact upon what will happen in the future. For Buddhists this means that this moment or the next will be influenced by the wholesome or unwholesome acts of the past.

The importance of rebirth and realms of existence is key to Buddhist teachings. What we are now and our present state is determined by what we thought or did in the past. What we are thinking and doing now will form the future states of being.

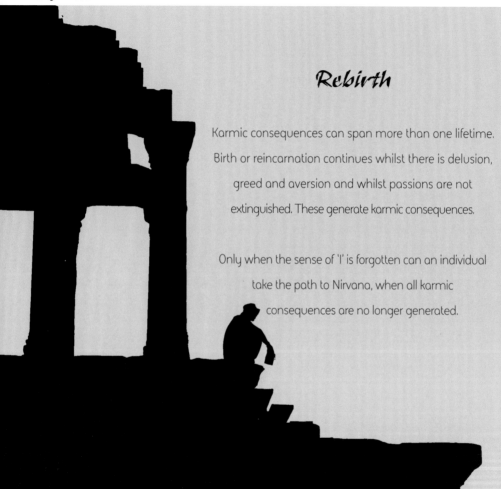

Rebirth

Karmic consequences can span more than one lifetime.
Birth or reincarnation continues whilst there is delusion,
greed and aversion and whilst passions are not
extinguished. These generate karmic consequences.

Only when the sense of 'I' is forgotten can an individual
take the path to Nirvana, when all karmic
consequences are no longer generated.

The Non-Self

Buddhism denies the existence of an immortal self or soul. Self is an illusion. Mind and body, feelings, perception, interpretations and consciousness are constantly changing and there is no abiding permanent entity.

The soul is an extension of the idea of the self and does not exist. Like a wave in the ocean, we are a temporary phenomenon.

Emptiness

Early Buddhism taught that there was no such thing as an enduring self or soul. As Buddhism developed, it was suggested that all phenomena could be seen to be empty of self or essence.

Emptiness, or Sunyata, suggests, therefore, that emptiness equates to Nirvana and the cessation of suffering.

The world is made up of ever-changing elements, or dharmas. The world is an illusion, a fabrication and the ultimate truth is the world as it really is, which is made up of mundane and super-mundane truth.

Through practice it is possible to let go of desire, anger and attachments and to be become calm and thus see the world as it really is, without delusion.

'Even emptiness itself, which is seen as the ultimate nature of reality, is not absolute, nor does it exist independently. We cannot conceive of emptiness as independent of a basis of phenomena, because when we examine the nature of reality, we find that it is empty of inherent existence.'

14th Dalai Lama, The Art of Living, *2001*.

Mandala Sand Paintings

Mandalas are geometric designs that are symbolic of the mind and the universe. Sand mandalas are constructed from sand by Tibetan monks to create a positive energy, both for the environment and those that view them.

It is said that the Buddha introduced sand painting. The process begins with an opening ceremony, during which the lamas consecrate the site. The mandala design is then marked with chalk on a wooden platform.

Monks use metal funnels to mark out the elaborate patterns in grains of dyed sand. When the mandala is completed the monks chant and begin the destruction of the mandala. It is then dispersed into flowing water and seen as a gift to re-energise the universe.

Theravada Buddhism

Theravada Buddhism

Theravada Buddhists strongly believe that their form of Buddhism is exactly how Buddha handed it down to them. It is a dominant religion in Sri Lanka, Myanmar and Thailand.

After spending several decades teaching, the Buddha had not written down any of his teachings. After his death a council of Buddhist monks was convened at Patna. They were concerned with what they saw as Buddhist heresies and sought to purify the religion. What came out of this council, to a great extent, was the definitive teachings of Theravada Buddhism. From that point onwards it has undergone limited change.

Theravada Origins

When the teaching of Buddha was finally written down they were written in a language derived from Sanskrit called Pali. The Pali scriptures became the definitive Theravada canon. They were probably written down 400 years after the death of Buddha, some think between 89 and 77 BC; others believe it was in the 1st century AD.

The basic doctrines of Theravada Buddhism are said to be the teachings of the Buddha. They are based on the Middle Way, the Four Noble Truths and the practice of the Noble Eightfold Path. It emphasises the importance of monastic life, ethical behaviour and meditation.

Expansion

Theravada Buddhism, often known as Southern Buddhism, became the dominant school of Buddhism in most of Southeast Asia from the 13th century AD. This coincided with the establishment of monarchies in Thailand, Myanmar, Cambodia and Laos.

Theravada Buddhism first appeared in Myanmar and Thailand in around AD 100. By the 13th century it had spread to Laos and Cambodia.

Before the late 19th century Theravada was little known outside of Southern Asia. In recent decades various Theravada schools and monasteries have sprung up across Europe and North America.

It is estimated that there are 61 million Theravada Buddhists in Thailand, 13 million in Sri Lanka and 12 million in Cambodia.

Theravada Beliefs

The Buddha warned against superstition and empty rituals, as they impede an individual's path. The only contact with the Buddha is through his teachings. God is a spiritual being but with limited powers and Buddha's teachings do but show the way, but making the journey is up to the individual.

The Supernatural

Unlike some other religions, Buddhism rejects the supernatural as meditation is used for awakening of enlightenment, not outside powers.

The Buddha

The Buddha was a man who became the awakened one and re-discovered an ancient path. For Buddhists he is not seen in the same way as Jesus is by Christians.

God

There is no creator, unlike in Christianity, Islam and Judaism. Gods exist, but are not omnipotent. They have limited powers and are impermanent.

The Path to Enlightenment

Everyone must make his or her own way to enlightenment. The Dharma is completely impersonal. Only Buddha's teachings show the way.

Theravada Life

Central to Theravada Buddhism is attaining self-liberation through one's own efforts. Ideally, individuals should dedicate themselves to full-time monastic life. But, by abstaining from evil and accumulating all that is good and purifying the mind, enlightenment can be found. This is achieved through practice.

Theravada Buddhist monks spend some of their time in meditation. How much depends on the time of the year and whether they are forest monks or live in the city. Once a person achieves liberation they become known as an 'Arhat' or 'Arahat'; a worthy person. Theravada Buddhism recognises that it is not possible for all to dedicate themselves to the monasteries and, as a result, there is a major role for lay followers in the religion and for monks to take part in the life of the community.

Theravada Monks

Theravada monks can join the community or Sangha as young as seven. It is possible to join the monastery at any time beyond that minimum age.

Novice monks are known as 'Samanera' and full monks are known as 'Bikkhu'.

Ordination begins with a formal request and the preparation for the ceremony by acquiring a complete set of robes. The applicant shaves their head and formally asks for the robes to be given by the senior monk.

The applicant makes a formal request for ordination and the senior monk administers the Three Refuges and the Ten Precepts.

Concepts and Practices

The monks take refuge in the Three Jewels, (Buddha, Dharma and Sangha) and accept the Ten Precepts. They are to abstain from taking life, from what is not given, from sexual contact, from false speech, use of intoxicants, food after midday, entertainment, perfumes and adornments, luxurious seats, taking or owning money.

In all, Theravada monks and nuns undertake the training or the Vinaya, consisting of 227 rules (with some additional ones for nuns).

Depending upon the Sangha, either five or ten Precepts form the basis of all of their training.

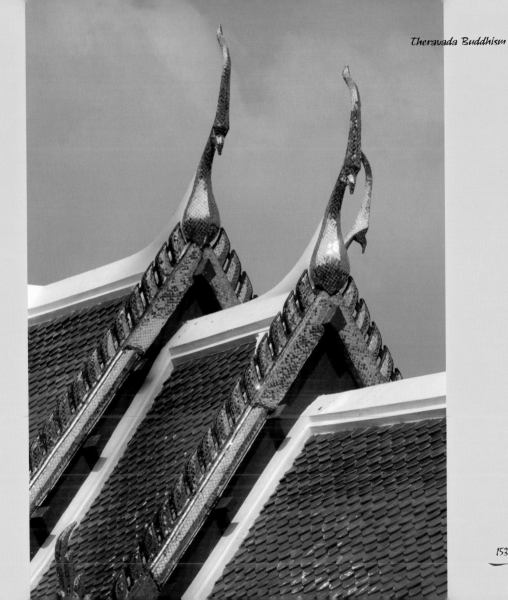

The Importance of Meditation

Meditation is extremely important, as it is a method for the cultivation of heart and mind. This cultivation emphasises concentration, clarity, calmness, insight and focus.

There are several different techniques and many of them are easy to learn and adaptable for use in daily life.

Theravada meditation stresses the importance of freeing the mind from mental distortions, such as greed, anger, stress, strain, despair and hatred. They believe that only once the mind is free from those mental distortions can the individual live a peaceful and blissful life. It is therefore of huge importance that the mind is trained.

Types of Meditation

There are two basic types of meditation in Buddhism. The first is known as Samatha and the other Vipassana. Meditation can only be undertaken under the guidance of a teacher, just as the Buddha did with his teachers

Samatha

Samatha is designed to calm the mind and heart, or to concentrate. It is used to cultivate the mind with the idea to end suffering. When this is practised, individuals focus on a single object of meditation. But most meditative objects are concepts. It is only after deep concentration that insight knowledge is built.

Vipassana

This is a form of meditation that is used to try to achieve insight into the true nature of things. Temporary changes are brought about by Samatha meditation, but the idea of Vipassana is to make permanent changes. It is designed to liberate the mind from all kinds of mental and physical suffering.

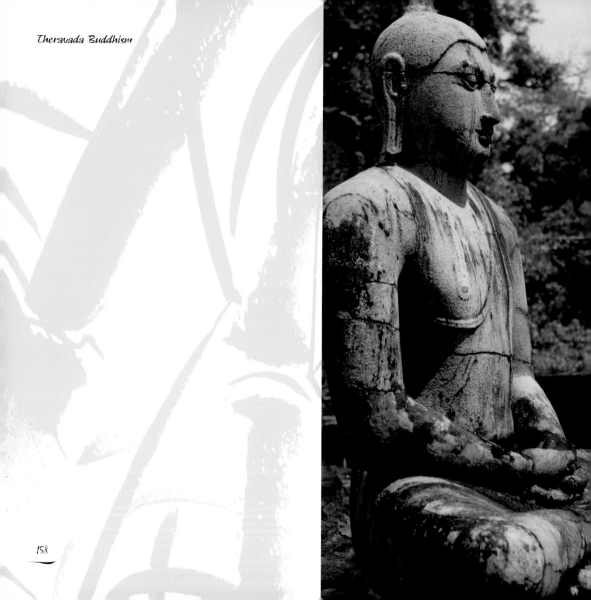

Insight Meditation

After someone has meditated for a considerable time, concentration becomes sharper and deeper. Finally, the mind can become absorbed by the object of meditation and it is absorbed into that object of meditation.

Once this state of mind has been achieved, this stage is called Jhana, which means 'fixed' or 'absorbed'. The mind becomes focused and as the individual continues to concentrate on subsequent occasions, the concentration and absorption becomes deeper and deeper.

There are many levels of absorption, or Jhanas, clearly described in the texts.

Meditation at Home

A person would need to find a time and a place, with a minimum amount
of distraction. Individuals usually set aside a period of time and begin to
meditate for just 15 minutes under the guidance of a teacher.

Meditation cannot be undertaken before the precepts are properly applied, and
there is proper moral discipline. Correct posture is very important, without which
the development of calm is impossible:. Many sit in the lotus position: the chin
is often tilted slightly down and the hands placed on the lap, palm upwards.

Individuals begin by collecting their attention, relaxing any tensions
and not allowing their mind to wander or daydream.

There are many different methods, from bare attention of the breath
to scanning the body: the method is left to the individual's teacher.

Theravada Buddhism

'Happy is the arising of a Buddha;

happy is the exposition of the Ariya Dhamma;

happy is the harmony amongst the Sangha;

happy is the practice of those in harmony.'

Dhammapada, v. 194

Anapanasati

This particular form of meditation is described in the 'awareness or mindfulness of breath' sutta. Sati means 'awareness', sometimes translated as 'mindfulness'.

The purpose is to become aware, while at the same time being careful not fall into a dazed state. By giving himself to the breath, the meditator notices when the mind has wandered and has to re-establish attention, this develops mindfulness/awareness, patience and insightful understanding of the nature of the mind, the body, the thoughts, feelings and impulses.

Most people use this because they get restless and agitated quite easily. They learn to be at peace with themselves, whilst paying complete attention to their body and posture and staying aware of their breath.

Further Cultivating the Heart/Mind

Cultivating goodwill or Metta gives another dimension to the practice of meditation. One purpose of meditation is to teach patience and tolerance, so as to develop a more friendly and caring attitude, both to yourself and to other people, thus mitigating the effects of the passions.

The person meditating thinks to themselves, 'may I be well', or 'may others be well', as they breathe in and out. They breathe in the qualities of tolerance and forgiveness, and breathe out stress, worry, negativity and problems.

The Relationship Between Monks and Lay People

Monks have a very strict code of behaviour, but they have a strong relationship with lay people. Theravada Buddhism could not exist without this form of interaction.

In return for food, medicine and cloth, the monks provide spiritual support, teaching and blessings.

Neither side can demand from the other. The spirit is more of openhearted giving. The system works well and the monks are normally well provided for, regardless of the poverty or the wealth of the locals in the area.

Throughout, the lay people follow the five basic Buddhist principles and live a less strict life than the Buddhist monks.

Festivals and Pilgrimages

There are several different commemoration days and ceremonies, including Wesak, marking the birth, enlightenment and passing away of the Buddha.

Retreats

Many monasteries have facilities for people to stay in retreat. Visitors are expected to abide by the Eight Precepts (abstention from killing, stealing, sexual activity, unskillful speech, drink, drugs, adornments, entertainments, luxury and eating after midday).

The accommodation is usually basic, but safe and adequate for meditation purposes.

Texts

The main teachings were collected in their final form in the 3rd century BC, following a Buddhist council at Patna in India.

Since they were written down in Sri Lanka in the 1st century AD, they have remained virtually unchanged.

Monks often learn sections of the texts by heart. They consider them to be the teachings of the Buddha. They are tools to help live lives, rather than divine revelations or absolute truths. The Buddha encouraged verification by practice.

The teachings were originally written down in Sri Lanka in Pali. There are three main sections, known as the Tipitaka, or 'three baskets'. They are also known as the Pali Canon or the Nikayas.

Vinaya Pitaka

These are the codes for monastic life, rules to be followed by Buddhist monks or nuns, who recite the 227 rules twice a month.

Sutta Pitaka

These are the teachings of the Buddha, the essence of Buddha's teachings, essential philosophy and ethics.

Abhidamma Pitaka

These are supplementary philosophic and religious teachings and commentaries. They complete the Tipitaka.

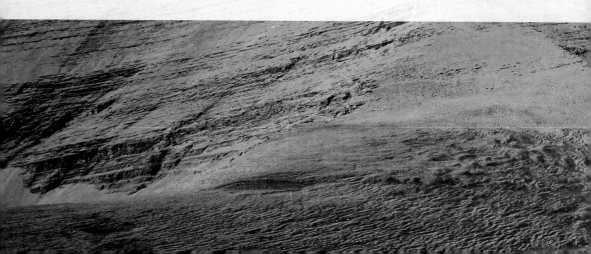

'Discipline is for the sake of restraint,

restraint for the sake of freedom from remorse,

freedom from remorse for the sake of joy,

joy for the sake of rapture,

rapture for the sake of tranquillity,

tranquillity for the sake of pleasure,

pleasure for the sake of concentration,

concentration for the sake of knowledge and vision of things as they are,

knowledge and vision of things as they are for the sake of disenchantment,

disenchantment for the sake of dispassion,

dispassion for the sake of release,

release for the sake of knowledge and vision of release,

knowledge and vision of release for the sake of total unbinding without clinging.'

Vinaya Pitaka: Parivara XII.2

Mahayana Buddhism

Mahayana Buddhism

Mahayana Buddhism

Mahayana Buddhists did not see themselves as creating new Buddhist doctrine, but quite the opposite. They believed that they were recovering the original teachings of the Buddha. These sutras are said actually to represent the further teachings not found in the original oral teachings.

The original oral teachings from which the present Theravada tradition was also derived (one of many schools at the time) are now lost.

Mahayana Buddhism teaches the Middle Way, the Four Noble Truths, the Noble Eightfold Path, the Three Fires, the Three Signs of Being and the Twelve-linked Chain of Dependant Arising, but represented a considerable departure, mainly because it declared that liberation was availble to all, monk and layman alike. At the same time it introduced other elements, including the idea of Buddahood and Bodhisattvas.

Mahayana Origins

Mainstream Indian Buddhism had centred on monastic life, leaving little room for the laity to attain liberation. A schism erupted in the 1st century BC, aimed to bring the teachings of Buddha to a larger number of people. The new Buddhism was called 'The Greater Vehicle', since it was designed to accommodate more people and more believers from different walks of life.

Mahayana Buddhism is now strongest in Tibet, China, Taiwan, Korea, Mongolia and Japan. It is not a single group, but a collection of traditions, which includes Zen, Pure Land and Tibetan.

All are Mahayana Buddhists and distinguishable from Theravada Buddhists.

Expansion

Mahayana Buddhism took around three centuries to reach a highly evolved form in China, by the 2nd century AD.

The first known scriptures were translations from Sanskrit made into Chinese, and the formal rise of the religion began in the 1st century AD, when it started to flourish and spread along the Silk Road from India to Central Asia, China, Korea and Japan. It disappeared from India during the 11th century due to the Muslim destruction of all Buddhism there. It lost much of its influence in Southeast Asia, particularly in Sri Lanka, where it was amalgamated with the Pali scriptures.

It has the largest number of adherents.

The Bodhisattva

Mahayana Buddhism is deeply concerned with the Bodhisattva, or the 'enlightenment being', who strives for the liberation of all sentient beings before seeking final release for themselves. They see this as an ideal way for a Buddhist to live. Anyone can embark on the path, as this is a way of life without selfishness. It incorporates a high regard for all beings, no matter what they are, and believes that they should be liberated from suffering.

般若心経 即説呪曰 羯諦羯諦波羅羯諦波羅僧羯諦菩提薩婆訶 一切苦真実不虚故説般若波羅蜜多呪 大明呪是無上呪是無等等呪能除

The Bodhisattva Vow

The Bodhisattva Vow encapsulates the credo by which Buddhists should live:

Sentient beings are innumerable, I vow to save them all. However inexhaustible the defilements are, I vow to extinguish them.

However immeasurable the teachings of the Dharma are, I vow to master them all.

However incomparable enlightenment is, I vow to attain it.

Avalokitesvara

This is the Bodhisattva of compassion. He is male in India but commonly regarded as female in China where she is called Kwan-yin. In Japan she is called Kannon or Kanzeon. Avalokitesvara is the attendant of Amitabha Buddha. In Tibet he is called Padmapani. He is quoted as saying:

'Throughout the samsaric world realms in the limitless space of the ten directions, I will benefit beings. I must liberate all beings from samsara. Not until all beings are established on the level of Buddhahood, not even one left behind in samsara, will I myself enter Buddhahood. Only when all beings without exception have been guided to Buddhahood, will it be well for me to achieve it. Until then I will remain in samsara for the benefit of all beings. And to ensure it, may my body be shattered into a thousand pieces if I break this vow.'

Manjushri

Manjushri is the Bodhisattva of supreme wisdom. He is regarded as the manifestation or idealization of the wisdom of the Buddha wisdom, intelligence and realisation. He is as popular a Bodhisattvas as Avalokiteshvara.

In Japan he is Monju-bosatsu: the name Manchuria is said to derive from his name. In Tibetan Buddhism he is sometimes shown as part of a trinity with Vajrapani and Avalokiteshvara.

He is depicted as a male wielding a flaming sword in his left hand. This represents his realisation of wisdom, cutting through ignorance and incorrect views. He carries the Prajnaparamita in his right hand. This represents his attainment of ultimate realisation and enlightenment.

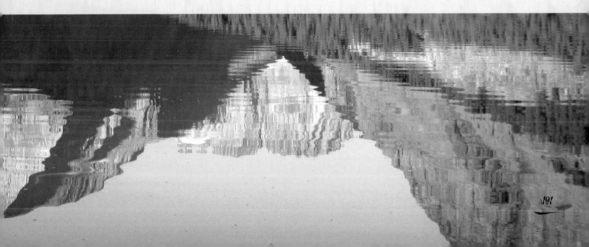

Maitreya

Maitreya is the Bodhisattva of future Buddha. Maitreya is who many Buddhists believe will eventually appear on Earth to achieve complete enlightenment.

Maitreya first appeared in Sanskrit text, stating that gods, men and other beings would worship Maitreya. He is often depicted as being seated, with both feet on the ground, indicating that he has not yet ascended to his throne. He is usually dressed in the clothes of Indian royalty. As a Bodhisattva, he will often be shown as standing and dressed in jewels. Sometimes his two acolytes, the great scholars and translators, Asanga and Vasubandhu, flank him.

Mahayana Buddhism

Bodhicitta

In Buddhist thought, Bodhicitta is the natural aspiration towards liberation for oneself and others. The word is a combination of Bodhi, or 'enlightenment', and Citta, meaning 'mind'. Therefore the word is sometimes translated as 'mind of enlightenment', or 'the spirit of altruism'.

The cultivation of Bodhicitta is one of the most important practices and can become selfless and unshakeable determination because the enlightenment is not for the individual, but for the benefit of everyone, or all living beings.

In Tibetan Buddhism there are various practices devoted entirely to this practice. In all schools of Buddhism the merit attained by any act is handed back to all sentient beings for the benefit of all.

Mahayana Buddhism

'Such compassion is not merely concerned with a few sentient beings such as friends and relatives, but extends up to the limits of the cosmos, in all directions and towards all beings throughout space'.

14th Dalai Lama

A Bodhicitta Prayer

Until I reach enlightenment, I take refuge in all the Buddhas,

And in the Dharma, and all the noble Sangha.

By the merit of accomplishing the six perfections

May I achieve Buddahood for the benefit of all sentient beings.

The Trikaya

The three bodies are three aspects of Buddhahood, according to Mahayana Buddhism:

Dharmakaya – Buddha is transcendent. He is the same as the ultimate truth, the manifestation of the Dharma itself that transcends all material and non-material things.

Sambhogakaya – Buddha's body of bliss or enjoyment body. This is how the Buddha appears in his own world, for the enjoyment of Bodhisattvas.

Nirmanakaya – Buddha's earthly body is just like any other human body. This is the Buddha who is the embodiment of the essence of Buddhist truth and ultimate reality.

Mahayana Buddhism

Extract from the Visualisation Sutra

This is an extract from the Visualisation Sutra:

'Blossoms and leaves are made of the seven kinds of jewels. Each blossom and leaf is the colour of a different jewel. From the lapis lazuli coloured blossoms is emitted a golden light; from the rock crystal coloured is emitted a crimson light; from the emerald coloured is emitted a sapphire light and from the sapphire coloured is emitted a pearl green ray of light. In addition, coral, amber and all the other myriad jewels serve as dazzling ornaments.'

The Dharmakaya

This is the truth or reality body by which the Buddha is of the nature of absolute reality beyond words and concepts.

The Sambhogakaya

Also known as the complete enjoyment body. The Buddha exists as a transcendental, eternal, celestial being or 'tangible' archetypal reality.

The Nirmanakaya

This is also known as the transformation or emanation body, or the visible, historical form of the Buddha.

The Pratyeka-Buddha

This is one of the three types of enlightened beings, said to have achieved enlightenment on their own. They do not teach.

The Arhant

This is a highly realised Buddhist, who has completely destroyed greed, hatred and delusion. In Tibetan this is a foe destroyer.

The Buddha Nature Doctrine

Buddha Nature relates to the possession of an innate
Buddha nature, which is not yet fully recognised or seen.
Buddha nature is incorruptible, uncreated and indestructible.
It is, in effect, eternal Nirvana, which opens up the possibility
of liberation from all suffering and impermanence.

Buddha nature is the union of wisdom and compassion
and is the essence of Buddahood. Even though it is
in everyone it is not obvious. It is obstructed by thoughts
and untransformed passions. Neither does it manifest
itself because of the various opinions blocking it.

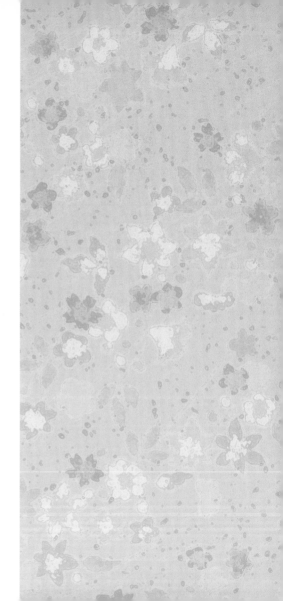

'What I call "being" is just a different name for this permanent, stable, pure and unchanging refuge that is free from arising and cessation, the inconceivable pure Dharmadhatu.'

14th Dalai Lama

The Origin of the Buddha Nature Doctrine

The Buddha Nature Doctrine can be traced back to a debate over metaphysics. Various schools tried to understand the problems of Buddhist psychology, such as 'what is the subject of karma and suffering and how do these processes occur', as well as the study of soteriology, the study of enlightenment.

The debates between the different schools provided the origination of Buddha nature. Buddha nature was not considered to be an isolated essence of a particular individual, but a single, unified essence, shared by all beings.

It is still a subject of enormous debate between parts of the Mahayana Buddhism schools.

Universalism

Simply, universalism suggests that everyone will become a Buddha. Once a Sravaka Buddha arises, he or she will direct others to the way to reach Nirvana, until there are no beings left in Samsara.

There is a difference between Mahayana Buddhism and Nikaya Buddhism, as the former does not say that a Bodhisattva will postpone Nirvana, whilst the latter says it will.

Mahayana Buddhists believe that Maitreya will be the next Buddha to manifest itself in this world and to introduce Dharma when it no longer exists.

The Lotus Sutra asserts that everyone will achieve total enlightenment and is therefore universal, whereas others suggest other routes to Nirvana, but not universal ones.

Enlightened Wisdom

According to Mahayana, traditional Buddhism tends still to focus on an individual attaining his or her own Nirvana. Mahayana Buddhists focus on Bodhicitta and with it a mind of great compassion, conjoined with wisdom. This will allow the Bodhisattva to work tirelessly for all living beings, until the follower will realise their goal of full enlightenment, or Buddahood, and be completely free of pointless suffering and its causes.

The six perfections (Paramitas or virtues), being generosity, patience, meditation, morality, energy and wisdom are practiced by all Buddhists of the Mahayana persuasion.

Most schools of Mahayana Buddhism concentrate on the practice of everyday life.

Compassion

A key consideration in Mahayana Buddhism is compassion. Followers believe that it is an indispensable element in the achievement of enlightened wisdom.

Compassion is an important aspect of Mahayana Buddhism. Unlike other Buddhist schools, Mahayanans believe that excess acquired merit can be transmitted to other individuals. The Bodhisattvas are considered to be the most compassionate. Avalokiteshvara (being an embodiment of supreme compassion) is the most compassionate of them all.

The Bodhisattvas, although they have reached enlightenment, show ultimate compassion by postponing their own entrance into Nirvana until all other beings have been saved. They show equal compassion in their devotion to help others reach enlightenment.

Liberation

In the Mahayana there are many Buddhas and Bodhisattvas which represent different aspects of ultimate reality. Used in meditation and other practices they aid the aspirant towards liberation.

Some sects believe that pure faith, or even by calling the Buddha's name, can obtain a rebirth into the pure land. Pure Land Buddhists often use mass devotional pleas for salvation.

Mahayana Buddhism has welcomed other faiths and their gods, bringing them into the rich tradition. These include popular Hindu devotional cults, Persian gods and Greco-Roman theology, all of which filtered into India from the north west.

Mahayana Buddhism

Texts

The first purely Mahayana scriptures were set in writing around the 1st century BC. Many of the teachings had only been passed down in the oral tradition and then remained hidden for several centuries. Among the earliest scriptures are the Perfection of Wisdom, the Avatamasaka Sutra, the Nirvana Sutra and the Lotus Sutra.

Many additional texts were added, including the Platform Sutra and the Sutra of Perfect Enlightenment. These were not of Indian origin, but still widely accepted.

Further developments in Korea and Japan brought forth additional commentaries, including those of the Korean Jinul and the Japanese Dogen.

'For the sake of all sentient beings, who are as infinite as space,

May I engage in the activity of the buddhas and bodhisattvas,

Without ever feeling discouraged or falling prey to laziness,

Always remaining joyful, with confidence and enthusiasm!'

14th Dalai Lama The Sage's Harmonious Song of Truth

Mahayanan Sutras

Mahayanan Sutras are a broad group of Buddhist scriptures, originally written in the 1st century BC, forming the basis of the varying Mahayana schools.

They believe that these are authentic accounts of the teachings given during the Buddha's life, with the exception of those of Chinese origin.

Generally, there are three categories, also known as the Turnings of the Wheel of Dharma. They are the early scriptures equivalent to the Pali Canon but in Sanskrit, and the two Mahayana turnings, the Prajna Paramita (perfection of wisdom) and the Tathagatagarbha (Buddha nature teachings).

According to Tibetan Buddhists, there are three categories. The Theravada Buddhists rely solely on the texts in Pali.

Pratyutpanna Sutra

The Pratyutpanna Sutra contains the first mention of the Buddha Amitabha and his Pure Land. It was first translated into Chinese between AD 178 and 189.

It is one of the earliest historically datable texts of the Mahayana tradition. It says:

'If you wish to come and be born in my realm, you must always call me to mind again and again, you must always keep this thought in mind without letting up, and thus you will succeed in coming to be born in my realm.'

The Pratyutpanna Sutra is also known as the Pratyutpanna Samadhi Sutra, which literally means 'the samadhi of being in the presence of all the Buddhas'.

Tibetan Buddhism

Tibetan Buddhism

Tibetan Buddhism is widely followed, not only in the Tibetan Plateau, but also in Mongolia, Siberia and other parts of Russia. Tibetan Buddhism is also gaining followers in Europe and America.

Tibetan Buddhism is a branch of Mahayana Buddhism. There are some Tantric and Shamanic features, along with material from an ancient Tibetan religion called Bon.

Many believe that Tibetan Buddhism is the same as Vajrayana Buddhism. On the contrary, Vajrayana Buddhism is taught as a part of Tibetan Buddhism, along with other schools of Buddhism.

History and Origins

It is believed that Buddhist scriptures arrived in southern Tibet from India in *c*. AD 173. It was the Tibetan king that had invited two Buddhist masters to his country and had important Buddhist texts translated into Tibetan.

Shantarakshita, an abbot from Nalanda, built Tibet's first monastery. Padmasambhava also came to Tibet and used his wisdom and power to overcome forces that were stopping work on the new monastery. He merged Buddhism with the local religion to create Tibetan Buddhism.

The new religion was to exert a strong influence from the 11th century across Central Asia, including Mongolia and Manchuria.

Tibetan Orders and Sects

Tibetan Buddhism has four main traditions. The oldest was founded by Padmasambhava and is known as the Nyingma (the ancient ones).

The Karmapa head the Kagyu (oral lineage). The Sakya Trizin head the Sakya (grey earth) and Ganden Tripa leads the Geluk (way of virtue). There is a further, minor one, in eastern Tibet called the Jonang.

There is a further movement known as the Rim and many count the Bon religion as a school of Buddhism, as it has completely assimilated Buddhist doctrine over the last thousand years. The Bon mythical founder was Tonpa Shenrab.

Tibetan Philosophical Schools

There are four main schools within the teachings. The first two are Hinayana-orientated and are known as the Vaibhasika and the Sautrantika, equivalent to the earliest sutra in Sanskrit, similar to the Pali Canon. The other two schools are Mahayana-orientated and are known as the Yogacara, or Chittamatra, and the Madhyamaka.

These philosophical schools were developed in India and each have their own sutras.

The philosophical differences are used in the monasteries and colleges to teach Buddhist philosophy in a systematic manner. The schools are each a gradual step and it is widely accepted that the Madhyamaka is the most sophisticated approach.

Special Features of Tibetan Buddhism

Tibetan Buddhism differs from other schools of Tantric Buddhism in three major ways. They believe in reincarnation lineages of certain Lamas and in a practice whereby lost or hidden ancient scriptures are recovered by spiritual masters. They also believe that a Buddha can be manifested in human form, such as Padmasambhava, who brought Tibetan Buddhism to the Himalayas.

Mythical figures have been incorporated into Tibetan Buddhism from the Bon religion and from Hinduism. They protect and uphold the Dharma. Many towns and districts have their own Dharma protector.

Tibetan Buddhism

Lamas

Tibetan Buddhism was often referred to as Lamaism. Lamas are religious teachers and central to the Buddhist doctrine and their institutions in the Himalayan region and in Tibet.

Certain Lamas have reincarnation lineages, known as Tulku. The most famous example of this is the Dalai Lama, who is said to be the reincarnation of the Bodhisattva Avalokitesvara. Believers are convinced that he has existed in 14 reincarnations since 1391.

Generally, Lama is a Tibetan title for a religious teacher. It is not applied to Tibetan monks generally, but does suggest spiritual attainment and an authority to teach.

Dalai Lamas

Tibetan Buddhists believe that the Dalai Lama can trace back their lineage to 1391. From the 17th century to 1959, the Dalai Lama was the head of the Tibetan government.

Dalai means 'ocean' in Mongolian and Lama is broadly the Tibetan equivalent to the Sanskrit word for 'spiritual teacher' guru. The title of Dalai Lama is more commonly translated as 'ocean of wisdom'.

On the death of the Dalai Lama, the hunt begins for his reincarnation, a small child. Familiarity with the possessions of the previous Dalai Lama is usually the main sign of the reincarnation. The search usually takes a few years.

List of Dalai Lamas

1st	Gedun Drub,	1391–1474
2nd	Gendun Gyatso	1475–1542
3rd	Sonam Gyatso	1543–88
4th	Yonten Gyatso	1589–1616
5th	Lobsang Gyatso	1617–82
6th	Tsangyang Gyatso	1683–1706
7th	Kelzang Gyatso	1708–57
8th	Jamphel Gyatso	1758–1804
9th	Lungtok Gyatso	1806–15
10th	Tsultrim Gyatso	1816–37
11th	Khendrup Gyatso	1838–56
12th	Trinley Gyatso	1856–75
13th	Thubten Gyatso	1876–1933
14th	Tenzin Gyatso	1935–present day

The Current Dalai Lama

The 14th and current Dalai Lama was born on 6 July 1935. Tenzin Gyatso, or in Tibetan, Bstan 'dzin Rgya Mtsho, was the fifth of nine children from a farming family in the Amdo Province of Tibet. He was proclaimed to be the reincarnation of the 13th Dalai Lama at the age of three. He was enthroned as Tibet's head of state on 17 November 1950.

Tibet faced occupation from China and when the Tibetan resistance movement collapsed in 1959, the Dalai Lama fled to India, where he set up a Tibetan government in exile.

The Karmapa Lama

The Karmapa Lama is the head of the Kagyu School, one of the four major schools of Tibetan Buddhism. The first Karmapa dates back to the 12th century. The current holder of the black crown or black hat is the 17th reincarnation, although there is dispute between two candidates.

Tantra

Tibetan Buddhism is highly influenced by Tantra. This has brought a wide range of rituals, symbols and techniques to the religion.

Tantra originated in India and is a common feature of both Buddhist and Hindu traditions. There are a number of associated spiritual techniques, including the use of mantras, mandalas, yoga and ceremonies and also visulisations.

Rituals

Meditation is an important part of Tibetan Buddhism. It is aided by hand gestures (mudras) and Mantras. Special cosmic diagrams, known as Mandalas, are created to assist inner spiritual development.

Lamas use a Dorje (translated as 'thunderbolt'), an eight-pronged ritual instrument which represents compassion and a hand bell (known as a Drilbu), which represents wisdom.

A Phurpa or ritual dagger is used symbolically to kill demons, releasing them for a better rebirth.

Merit can be gained by performing rituals, including offerings of food, flowers and water. Additional merit can be gained from religious pilgrimages or chanting prayers and lighting butter lamps.

Ritual Traditions

Tibetan villagers take part in Cham dances. The dancers wear masks and ornamental costumes. They perform the sacred dance to music played by monks on traditional instruments. The dances are designed to give instruction about not harming sentient creatures.

Tibetan ceremonies are generally noisy and visually appealing. They make use of brass instruments, gongs and symbols, which all take place in striking temples and monasteries.

Advanced spiritual techniques are used, with deep meditation. Senior Tibetan yoga experts can control their body temperature and heart rate.

Many of the rituals are very advanced and are designed for those that have a sophisticated understanding of the spiritual practice.

Festivals and Celebrations

In Bhutan, dances are performed at an annual festival called Tsechu. Other festivals feature a large painting, known as a Thongdrol. By glimpsing the painting an individual can carry enough merit to absolve them from all present sin. At present, the Chinese occupation force in Tibet prohibits Cham dances.

Prayer Wheels and Flags

The Tibetans call their prayer wheels Mani wheels. These are wheels on a spindle and on each wheel is written prayers or Mantras. Spinning the wheel has the same effect as reciting the prayer.

Prayer flags are cotton cloth squares in blue, green, red, white and yellow. There are two kinds of prayer flags: horizontal ones and vertical ones.

In the centre of a prayer flag there is an image of a wind horse, bearing the three jewels of Buddhism.

Tibetans believe the prayers will be blown upwards as offerings and will bring benefit to any that hang the flags.

Mantras

A mantra is a short phrase or prayer, which is either spoken once or repeated over and over again. The mantra is said to have a strong spiritual effect. It is usually common practice to use prayer beads to mark the number of repetitions.

Mantras can also be displayed on prayer wheels or written on prayer flags. In the former repetition is achieved by spinning the wheel and in the latter it is repeated each time the flag moves in the wind.

Prayer devices are very common and can be tiny or vast objects, up to 2.7 m (9 ft) high.

Avalokiteshvara's Mantra:

'Om mani padme hum' (Behold the jewel in the lotus)

Mandalas

The Mandala is essentially a symbolic picture of the mental universe. In some cases it can be a painting on a wall, or an illustration on a scroll. It can also be created in coloured sands on a table, or simply be visualised in the mind.

The centre of a mandala is used during meditation as an object to focus attention. When created in sand, it is used to symbolise impermanence. It can take days or weeks to create the intricate pattern, but once this is done, the sand is brushed together and then placed into running water to spread the blessings of the mandala.

Death and Impermanence

The awareness of death and impermanence is an important aspect of Tibetan Buddhism. In common with all Buddhist traditions and schools, they stress that everything is in the process of change; even a human body's cells are changing. This helps remind followers of their own impermanence.

Tibetan Buddhists do not believe that this awareness should produce despair or sadness, neither should it induce the individual to pursue the pleasure in their short lives. Instead, followers are encouraged to value every second of existence, to meditate and follow strict religious practice.

The awareness of death and the good fortune to be born as a human being helps lead Buddhists to understand that only spiritual things will last.

Preparing for Death

Tibetan Buddhists use exercises and visual meditation to imagine death and prepare for the Bardo (the state between death and rebirth).

They try to gain an understanding and an acceptance of death as being part of an inevitable journey. By understanding Bardo, an individual can help the dead and also themselves to gain a better experience of Bardo before they enter into it themselves.

The idea is to have a consciousness of Bardo. But for those who cannot achieve this, they will have at least achieved a greater experience regarding the impermanence of every living thing around them, including themselves.

Tibetan Book of the Dead

The Tibetan Book of the Dead is, in fact, the English title of one of the great texts of Tibetan Buddhism. It is a strong seller throughout the world and the book's real name is *Great Liberation* (through hearing during the intermediate state). More commonly, it is known as 'liberation through hearing'.

Bardo

Bardo is a Tibetan word that literally means
'intermediate state'. It can also be known as
'in between state' or 'transitional state'.
It refers to the state of existence between
two lives on Earth. After death, but before
the next birth, an individual's consciousness
is not connected to a physical body and
experiences new phenomena. Sometimes
these will be clear experiences of reality,
terrifying hallucinations or other sights.

For those who are spiritually advanced, it is
believed that Bardo is liberating, as it provides
transcendental insights and the ability to
directly experience reality. Hallucinations
can foretell a less than desirable rebirth.

Padmasambhava

Padmasambhava founded the Tibetan or Tantric School of Buddhism. He is also known as Guru Rinpoche, or Precious Master.

Followers of the Nyingma School consider him to be the second Buddha.

He established his reputation by his ability to memorise and understand esoteric texts after just one hearing. He was accused of killing an evil minister and banished from the court.

He developed the power to transcend the cycle of birth and death and his fame drew the attention of the 38th king of Tibet, at a time when Tibet was under attack from evil deities.

Padmasambhava Comes to Tibet

Padmasambhava used his Tantric powers to deal with the evil gods he encountered in Tibet. He founded Tibet's first monastery, called Samye Gompa. He is also associated with the Taktshang, or Tiger's Nest monastery, built 500 m (1,640 ft) above the Paro Valley. He flew here from Tibet on his consort, who had transformed herself into a flying tigress.

Padmasambhava's body print can be found on the wall of a cave close to the Kurje Lhakhang Temple in the Bumthang District.

Padmasambhava hid several treasures and hidden texts around Tibet for them to be later translated and interpreted. They are believed to be in fields, forests, caves and lakes around the Himalayas.

The Manifestations of the Padmasambhava

Padmasambhava is said to have taken eight forms, representing different aspects of his being:

– Padmavajra, Vajra of the Lotus severed the roots of the five poisons

– Padmaraja, King of the Lotus, provided the ultimate benefits to sentient beings

– Padmasambhava, the Lotus Born, blessed beings endowed with faith

– Dorje Droled, tamed the Yakshas and haughty beings

– Suryap Rabha, the Rays of the Sun, taught the essence of Secret Mantra

– Sakyasimha, the Lion of Sakyas, guided beings towards the path of liberation

– Simhanada, Roar of the Lion, defeated the outside aggressors of non-Buddhists

– Dhimanvaruchi, the Supremely Wise Love, showered the teaching of Sutra and Mantra.

Chanting

Chanting is the traditional way of preparing the mind for meditation and plays a substantial role in Buddhism. It is used in rituals to set the mind on a deity, mandala or concept. The chant 'om mani padme hum' is a chant used in praise of peace and the primary mantra of Avalokitesvara.

Medicine Buddha

Bhaisajyaguru, or Bhaisajyaguruvaiduryaprabha, is also known as the master of healing, or the medicine Buddha. The literal full translation is 'medicine master lapis lazuli light'.

The medicine Buddha fulfilled 12 vows and two of them related to healing. When he reached Buddahood he became the Buddha of a realm where he was attended by the Bodhisattvas Nikko and Gakko.

He is usually depicted seated, wearing monk's robes and often has a blue-coloured jar of medicine in his left hand. His right hand rests on his right knee and between his thumb and first finger is the stem of the Aurara plant.

'If one meditates on the Medicine Buddha,
one will eventually attain enlightenment,
but in the meantime one will experience
an increase in healing powers both for
oneself and others and a decrease in
physical and mental illness and suffering.'

Lama Tashi Namgyal

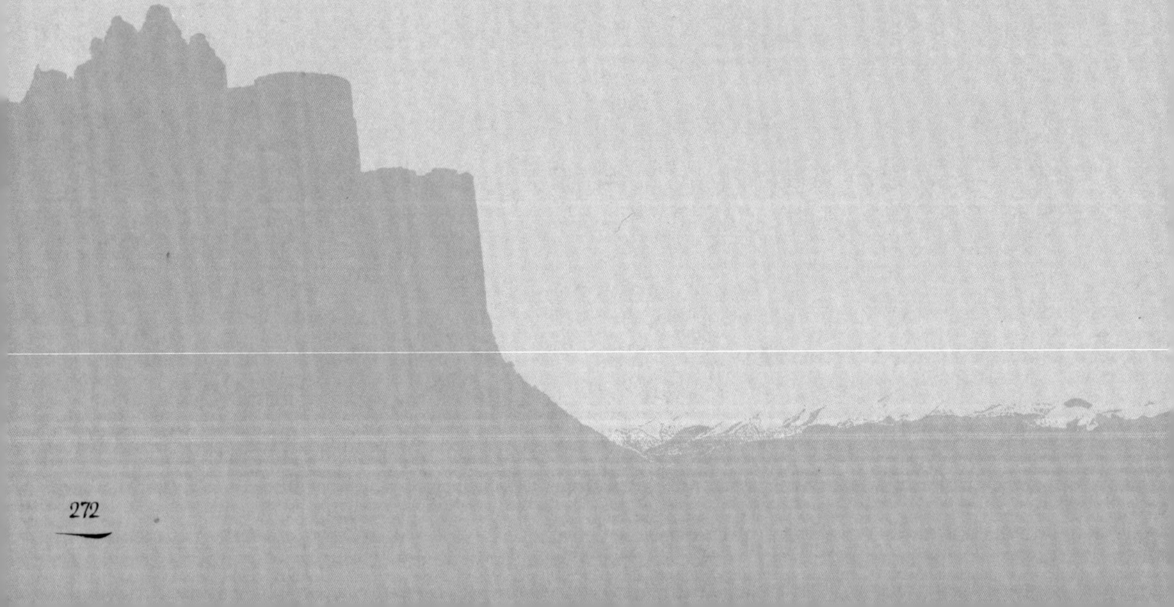

'His radiant body is azure blue. His left hand is in the meditation mudra and holds a begging bowl full of long life nectar in his lap. As a sign that he gives protection from illness, his right hand is outstretched in the gesture of giving and holds the "great medicine", the myrobalan plant (a-ru-ra).'

Men-Tse-Khang

Zen Buddhism

Zen Buddhism

Zen Buddhism

The word Zen is a Japanese transliteration of the word *ch'an*, which is in itself a transliteration of the word *dhyana*, a Sanskrit word meaning absorption or meditation. It is thus the meditation school of Buddhism based on the core teachings of the Buddha; the Middle Way , the Four Noble Truths, the Three Signs of Being, the Three Fires, the Twelve-Linked Chain of Dependant Arising.

The primary goal of Zen is liberation in this lifetime, a teaching outside the scriptures, non-reliance on words and phrases, a direct pointing to the human heart and becoming Buddha. .

Zen is a Mahyana way: it is extremely disciplined, but this discipline results in spontaneity, naturalness and freedom, but not impulsiveness.

History and Origins

Bodhidharma was an Indian monk who brought Zen Buddhism to China in the 6th century. It was known as *Ch'an* in China.

Ch'an's true golden age began in the period AD 638 to 713 and ended when Buddhists were persecuted in China during the middle of the 9th century AD.

Many of the key Zen masters come from this period and although Ch'an Buddhists were persecuted, they survived, but never at the level known before.

Zen came to Korea in the 7th century where it was called Seon, and Japan five centuries later. Zen was popularised in the West by the Japanese scholar, Daisetz Teitaro Suzuki (1870–1966).

Shinto

Shinto is the ancient religion of Japan. It was made the state religion in 1868 following the Meiji restoration and involves the worship of sacred spirits, which take the form of wind, rain, trees, rivers and other things and concepts. After the Second World War it lost its status as the state religion when the emperor renounced his status as a living god.

Buddhism was affecting Shinto following its adoption by the court. Buddhism had been rapidly assimilated. Many believed that the Kami, or spirits, were just Buddha by another name. The two religions co-existed and there was an attempt to amalgamate them in Shinbutsu Shugo. In 1868 this combination with Buddhism was outlawed.

Bodhidharma

He was said to be the man who brought Zen Buddhism from India to China. After having had a very famous meeting with the Chinese Emperor, Bodhidharma spent the next six years facing a wall, deep in meditation. On one occasion he fell asleep and to keep awake he cut off his eyelids and threw them to the ground. The first tea plants sprouted from the spot.

On another occasion, so legend has it, he sat in meditation for so long that his legs fell off. Round-bottomed dolls that do not fall over were designed to communicate his spirit:

'Such is life

Seven times down

Eight times up.'

Enlightenment is Inside

Zen Buddhists believe that all human beings are Buddhas and all that is required of them is to discover that truth.

Zen Buddhists seek liberation, but know it cannot be found by philosophy, rational thought, rituals or scriptures alone. It can be found, however, through practice and meditation, letting go and giving up anxious speculative thinking.

Zen Buddhists believe that they do not need to search outside themselves for answers; the answer is in the same place as the question.

Zen Buddhism

Zazen

Zazen is an important aspect of Zen Buddhist meditational practice. It is a Japanese concept that literally means 'seated concentration'. The idea is to calm the body and mind and thereby gain an insight into the nature of existence.

It was originally conceived as a seated meditational exercise, but can now be used in any posture. The individual breathes naturally without special effort, half lowers their eyelids, so that they are neither open nor shut, in order to stay awake.

Traditionally Zazen is performed on a mat called a Zabuton, whilst sitting on a cushion called a Zafu.

Sitting Meditation

Common seating positions for Zazen include the:

- Kekkafuza (full lotus)
- Hankafuza (half lotus)
- Burmese (cross-legged with the ankles placed together in front of the sitter)
- Seiza (kneeling using a bench or Zafu)
  Seated comfortably upright in a chair,
  to maintain the natural curve of the spine

Seeking Enlightenment

The essence of Zen Buddhism is to achieve enlightenment by focusing on the breath or using various meditational subjects such as koans, without the intervention of the picking and choosing intellect.

It is concerned with what actually is rather than what is thought or felt. To be truly human is to be a Buddha. Buddha nature is just another name for human nature in its pure state, unclouded by selfishness and personal anxieties.

Rinzai School

The Rinzai School is one of the major Japanese Zen sects. It is the Japanese branch of the Chinese Linji School and was brought to Japan in 1191.

It is divided into 15 branches, organised by the name of their head temples.

Rinzai is known for its emphasis on sudden enlightenment and the use of koan.

The Samurai cast adopted Rinzai, because the practice helped remove the fear of death, and because it required so much self discipline. It was said to have been believed at the time 'Rinzai for the Shogun and Soto for the peasants'.

Soto School

Soto is a Japanese Zen school and a branch of Chinese Caodong, brought to Japan by Dogen Zenji. It is the largest Zen sect in Japan, with 14,700 temples and 7 million believers.

Soto's roots go back to the mountain area of the Hunan Province in China. There are similarities to the traditions of Tibetan Buddhism, where a senior monk becomes a lineage bearer in a Dharma Transmission ceremony. The monk will have already be throughly settled and lived for some decades in a Zen monastery.

The lineage documents of all Zen schools trace all the way back to the Buddha, the historic founder of Buddhism.

Zen Buddhism

Martial Arts

The Rinzai School is closely associated with the martial arts tradition in Japan. Rinzai was popular among the warrior and Samurai classes. Zen training aims to remove all fear of death and for a warrior the fear of death was a natural obstacle.

Zen practice was therefore essential for warriors. Its emphasis on literature and intellectual knowledge also attracted the educated and literate classes.

Rinzai Zen was formally introduced to the warrior cast in Kamakura in 1199. The popularity continued until the late 19th century and directly led to the development of Bushido as a regular training for the warrior cast.

koan Practice

Koans are stories, dialogues, questions or statements. They usually contain aspects that are not immediately clear but may be accessible to some.

Koans are originally sayings, or doings of legendary figures. Monks, teachers and students in training use them. There are not necessarily fixed answers to each koan.

Tea Ceremony

The Japanese tea ceremony is very closely associated with
the Rinzai School. It was almost certainly brought over
to Japan from China, along with the concept of mixing
powdered green tea with hot water. By the 15th century,
it had become a prominent part of Japanese culture.

The tea ceremony is gives a flavour of doing a very
ordinary act with complete relaxed attention, that
involves the whole person and all their senses.
Most of what we do involves simple tasks but we
normally are fully conscious of what we are doing.

Calligraphy

Calligraphy using hanging scrolls is important in the tea ceremony. Scrolls written by Buddhist monks, artists or famous calligraphers, are hung in the scroll alcove of the tearoom. They are often chosen for their appropriateness in relation to the theme of the ceremony, the time of day or the season.

They feature well known sayings, poems, descriptions, words or phrases, either associated with Buddhism or directly with the tea ceremony. Typically characters depicting harmony, purity, respect and tranquillity may be used. A rabbit, for example, might be used for an evening ceremony due to its association with the moon.

Sometimes scrolls are also placed in the waiting room outside the tearoom.

Flower Arranging

A form of flower arrangement associated with tea ceremonies is called Chabana. It has roots with other forms of Japanese flower arranging, which in turn have roots in Buddhism and in Shinto.

The original flower-arranging tradition was known as Ikebana and used by the earliest tea masters. Chabana now provides a standard style of arrangement for tea ceremonies. It usually involves a simple arrangement of seasonal flowers in a unadorned container. They will usually only have a few stems and these are often put into tall, narrow vases made from natural materials, including ceramics, metal and bamboo.

Bankei

Bankei Yotaku (1622–93) was a 17th century Japanese Zen master. He was a Rinzai priest and renowned for his teachings. He gave orders that no one should write down his words, as they would be diminished. His followers were beside themselves that their masters' words would be lost so they ignored him.

Bankei delivered sermons in plain, everyday Japanese. No one before him had brought Zen Buddhism to the ordinary people in such a thorough and accessible manner.

306

'You are aware of your Buddha-minds
because they're covered by illusions and
can't be seen. But you never lose them,
not even when you go to sleep. The unborn
Buddha-mind that your mothers have
given you is thus always there, wonderfully
clear and bright and illuminating.'

Bankei Yotaku

Hakuin Ekaku

Hakuin Ekaku (1686–1769) was one of the most influential figures in Japanese Zen Buddhism. The Rinzai School was declining and he transformed it with a focus on meditation and Koan practice.

He was born at the foot of Mount Fuji and at the age of 15 he was ordained at a local Zen temple. He became an abbot in his early thirties and at 41 he experienced enlightenment after reading the Lotus Sutra.

He spent the next 40 years writing and teaching and built up a large community of monks, transforming Hara into the centre of Zen teaching by his death at the age of 83.

Dogen Zenji

Dogen Zenji (1200–53) was an important religious figure and philosopher and a teacher and founder of the Soto School in Japan.

His parents had died young, which helped him understand the meaning of impermanence and inspired him to become a monk. Over the years he studied and sought the truth and in 1244 he established a temple, which remains an important centre for the Soto School to the present day.

He wrote and taught. His poetry and use of language was unconventional. Together with his successor, Keizan, they are the joint founders of the Soto School.

Zen Buddhism

'To study the Way is to study the self. To study the self is to forget the self. To forget the self is to be enlightened by all things. To be enlightened by all things is to remove the barriers between oneself and others.'

Genjokoan, Dogen Zenji

Ryokan

Ryokan (1758–1831) was a Zen Buddhist monk who lived in Niigata in Japan. He left the monastery and lived as a hermit, until old age forced him to live in the house of one of his followers.

Ryokan was particularly famed for his calligraphy and poetry. He loved children and often forgot to walk around with his alms bowl because he was playing with the children from a nearby village.

His poetry is considered simple and is heavily inspired by nature. He never really accepted his position as a priest or even a poet, because of his extreme humility.

Ryokan's Poetry

Ryokan shows a sense of humour and refuses to take himself too seriously in his quotes and in his poetry. His poems give interesting insights into the practice of Zen. He lived a pure and simple life and there were many stories relating to his generosity and kindness. His deathbed poem was:

'Showing their backs
Then their fronts
The autumn leaves scatter in the wind.'

Dewdrops on a Lotus Leaf:

'The wind has settled, the blossoms have fallen;

Birds sing, the mountains grow dark —

This is the wondrous power of Buddhism.'

Also from Ryokan:

'The Three Thousand Worlds that step forward with the light snow,

And the light snow that falls in those Three Thousand Worlds.'

Paramitas

There are six guiding paramitas (perfections) that Zen Buddhists strive to achieve. These are the perfection or culmination of practices cultivated by Bodhisattvas to pass from a strenuous life to enlightenment. These are:

- The Dana Paramita — giving
- The Shila paramita — morality
- The Ksahnti paramita — forbearance
- The Virya paramita — joyful energy
- The Dhyana paramita — settled, focused meditation
- The Prajna paramita - knowledge.

Important Soto Texts

There are a number of important texts that
express Soto Zen Buddhism and these are
often chanted in temples to this day.

Extract from *The Harmony of Difference and Sameness*

'The mind of the great sage of India is

intimately transmitted from west to east.

While human faculties are sharp or dull, the

Way has no northern or southern ancestors.

The spiritual source shines clear in the light;

the branching streams flow on in the dark.

Grasping at things is surely delusion, according

with sameness is still not enlightenment.

All the objects of the senses transpose and do not transpose.

Transposing, they are linked together;

not transposing, each keeps its place'

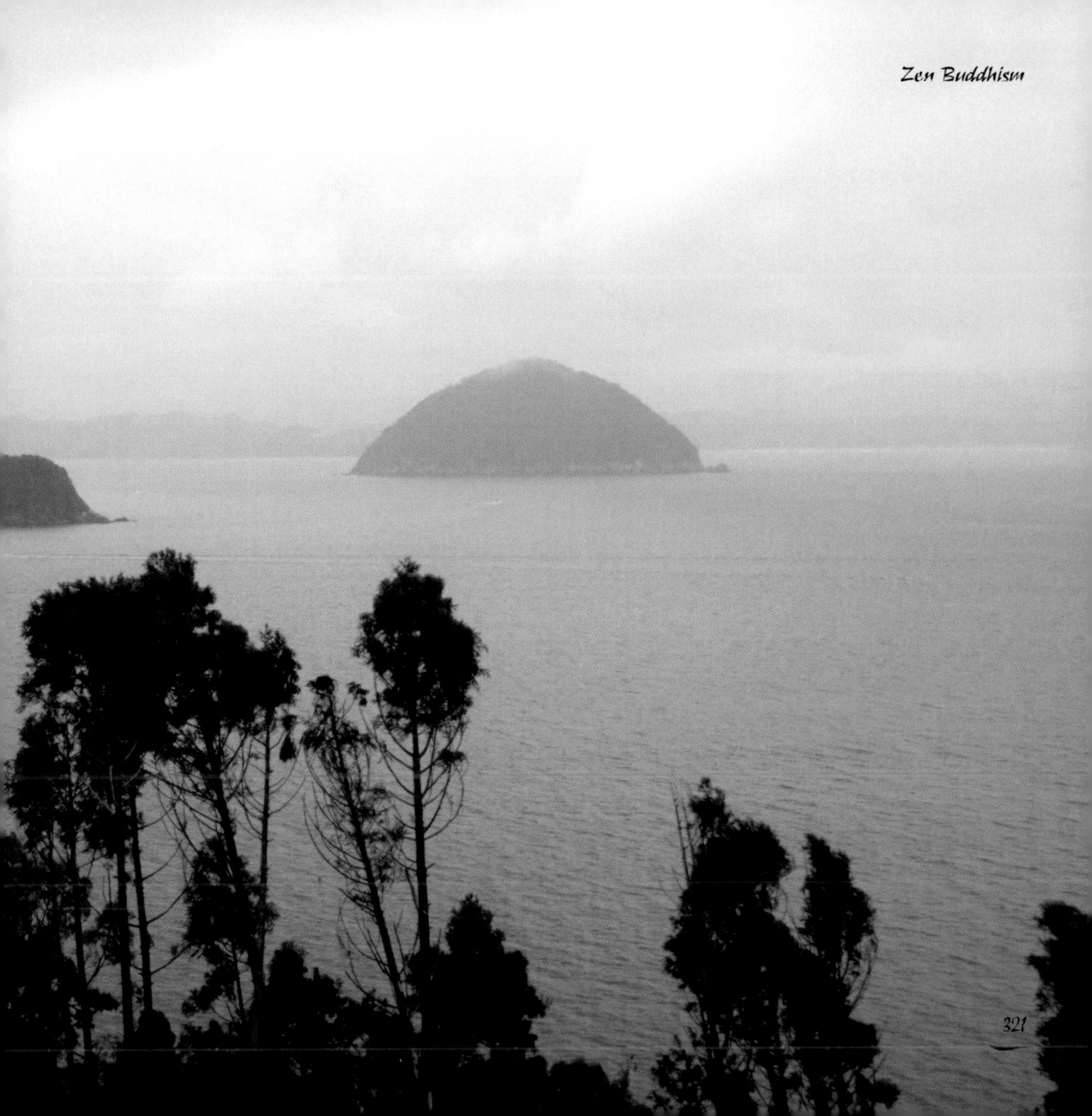

Zen Buddhism

Extract from *The Song of the Jewel Mirror Awareness*

'The Dharma of thusness

Is intimately conveyed by Buddhas and Ancestors;

Now you have it,

Keep it well.

Filling a silver bowl with snow,

Hiding a heron in the moonlight —

When you array them, they're not the same;

When you mix them, you know where they are.

The meaning is not in the words,

Yet it responds to the inquiring impulse'

Shobogenzo

Shobogenzo, or *Treasury of the True Dharma Eye*, is a collection of Zen Buddhist fascicles, written by Dogen Zenji. They were written in Japanese rather than Chinese. Up until that point most Zen writings that had originated in Japan had been written in Chinese.

The modern edition contains 95 fascicles, although earlier collections had between 28 and 75. The writer himself believed that only 12 of these essays were actually complete.

They are often used as sermons. Not all were written by Dogen and were recorded by his disciples from his oral sermons. Not all the fascicles have as yet been translated into English.

Honkyoku Music

Honkyoku are pieces of Shakuhachi or Hocchiku music.
Japanese Zen monks, known as Komuso, often played
these. They played the Honkyoku in exchange for alms
and provided enlightenment, possibly as early as the
13th century. There are various different teaching
methods, with varying styles and emphasis, delivered
by Honkyoku schools, also known as Ryu.

Buddhism Today

Buddhism Today

There are said to be 396 million Buddhists worldwide. The vast majority of Buddhists practice the traditions into which they were born, observe festivals, take part in the regular celebrations, are married, die and are consigned to future birth as Buddhists. In the West, however, Buddhism has only recently gained popularity.

Buddhism is attractive as it dispenses with the notion of a supreme being, as does science. It provides everything that other religions offer: devotion; the spiritual life; ztransformation of the heart and mind; and the practice of wisdom and compassion, without the necessity of blind belief in a revealed text or supernatural creator god. It is never in conflict with science, in fact seems in agreement with it at a profound level.

Buddhism in the West

The spiritual void created by the slaughter of hundreds of millions of people in the last century, the revelations of science, materialism, leisure, education and intense questioning has given rise to a thirst for something other than the traditional solutions to the spiritual quest.

Buddhism is one of the fastest-growing religions in the Western world. Small groups of committed Western Buddhists, now supported by Japanese, Korean, Chinese and other Buddhist communities from a variety of different countries, including Tibet, are living Buddhist lives. Apart from the main traditions practiced here there are other new movements, such as Engaged Buddhism and the Western Buddhist Order.

Buddhism Comes to Europe

The great scholars who went out to India such as William Jones, Sir Alexander Cunningham and others contributed in discovering the origins of Buddhism in India. The French translator Eugène Burnouf produced new scholarship.

German scholars, as well as the great philosopher Arthur Schopenhauer, spread the influence of Buddhism ever further. The British scholar, T. W. Rhys Davids, founded the Pali Text Society and made the Pali Canon available in English.

The Light of Asia (1891) by Sir Edwin Arnold had worldwide appeal and made Buddhism popular amongst the educated.

The theosophists Madame Helena Blavatsky and Henry Steel Olcott visited Sri Lanka in 1880 were partly responsible for the Buddhist revival there.

Buddhism Takes Root

Englishman Allen Bennett went to Myanmar in 1901 to learn about Buddhism first hand and returned a year later as Venerable Ananda Metteya, a convert to the Theravada tradtion (although he later disrobed). Anton Gueth from Germany became Venerable Nyanatiloka in 1903 and founded in the Island Hermitage in Sri Lanka in 1911 as a monastery devoted to training Western monks.

Throughout the early twentieth century, Buddhist societies were founded: the Buddhist Society in London in 1924 and the Berlin Buddhist Society the same year. Popular publications and translations of all kinds also started to appear.

Buddhism in Britain

Sri Lankans

The London Buddhist Vihara in Knightsbridge opened in 1954.
In 1990 the Vihara was taken over by Venerable Vajiragnana,
a notable scholar and speaker.

Thais

The Bhuddhapadipa temple opened in 1966; since 1975 it
has been located in Wimbledon. The first incumbent was
the Venerable Sobhana Dhammasudhi, who later disrobed
and went to the USA to teach meditation.

Myanmarese

They opened their first Vihara in Birmingham in 1978.
The first incumbent was Venerable Dr Rewata Dhamma,
a scholar of both Theravada and Mahayana Buddhism.

The British Theravadins

Besides Allen Bennett, there was Osbert Moore who went to Sri Lanka, was ordained as Bhikkhu Nyanamoli and trained under Nyanatiloka at Pilgrim's Island, where he translated suttas until his premature death. Lawrence Mills also ordained as Bhikkhu Khantipalo. He then worked in India before going to Australia and establishing two temples before disrobing.

The English Sangha Trust was founded in 1955. It was set in motion by William Purfurst who became Bhikhhu Kapilavuddho in Thailand before returning to England. He returned to Thailand but later disrobed due to ill health. He ordained Alan James, who went on to found Aukana, a Theravada trust and meditation community.

The British Sangha

Ajahn Sumedho first came to Buddhism as Robert Jackman. He was trained by Ajahn Chah from north-east Thailand in the forest tradition. In the late 1970s, Ajahn Sumedho established the Cittaviveka Forest Monastery at Chithurst in West Sussex, which was the first substantial community for monks and nuns in Britain.

In 1981 Harnham was founded near the Scottish border and Devon in 1983. Amaravarti, a vast network of monasteries and hermitages, was established in 1984, and has now spread to Switzerland, Italy, the USA, New Zealand and Australia.

Buddhism Today

Tibetan Buddhism

The only good thing to result from the invasion of Tibet by Chinese forces in 1949 is that Tibetan Buddhism has come to the West. After the Dalai Lama was forced to flee his country in 1959, the Indian government provided a haven for the Tibetan government-in-exile in Dharamsala, a former hill-station

Almost 80,000 Tibetans followed and brought with them their deep faith and belief in Buddhism. Many learned monks were given asylum in Europe and America; many of these monks were abbots of their own monasteries in Tibet and were men of great ability.

The story of Tibetan Buddhism in England has been one of amazing success. In a relatively short time it has become thoroughly established with many monasteries, centres and retreat houses.

kagyu Samye Ling

This is the name of the first Buddhist monastery in Tibet. It is also the name of the first Tibetan Buddhist monastery in the United Kingdom and still remains one of the biggest in Europe, founded by Akong Tulku Rinpoche in 1967. They also own Holy Island off the west coast of Scotland.

There are many centres in London and all the major cities in the UK; all the Tibetan schools are represented and the numbers of practicing English and European Tibetan Buddhists is increasing year on year.

karma kagyu Marpa House

This was established by Chime Rinpoche in 1973 and is a retreat house run for the benefit of all.

Zen Buddhism in Britain

Zen Buddhism came to Britain rather later than the other traditions.

Mr Christmas Humphreys established a friendship with the writer and translator D.T. Suzuki while in Japan which led to not only the publication of many books on Zen, but also coincided with a sudden interest in Zen Buddhism throughout the western world. Several communities have since been established.

Buddhism in America

The first Buddhist temple in America was built in 1853 by the SzeYap Company (a Chinese-American fraternal society) to help Chinese workers in America. Originally called Joss Houses by Americans, there were eight temples by 1875 and then almost 400 by 1900.

Japanese immigration gave rise to the first temple in Hawaii in 1896 in the Jodo Shinshu School.

Jodo Shinshu is a branch of the Pure Land School founded by Shinran, a student of Honen. The central belief is one of reliance on 'other power' — that of Amida Buddha's — through the recitation of 'Namu Amida Butsu' ('I take refuge in Amida Buddha'). This particular school has a large following in Japan and throughout the world.

The Dial

Ralph Waldo Emerson's literary magazine, *The Dial*, published parts of the Lotus Sutra in 1844, translated from Eugène Burnouf's French translation into English by Elizabeth Peabody. This influenced many Americans, including Walt Whitman.

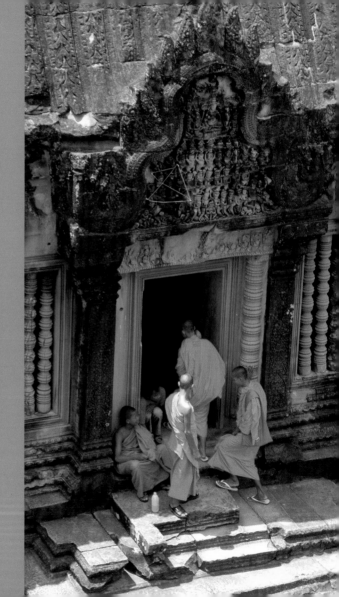

The Parliament of World Religions

Held in 1893, this was probably the most important event to occur in America in the 19th century as far as Buddhism was concerned. It was Buddhism's first public forum, due to so many attending the event and its extensive covering by the press. A notable attendee was Henry Steel Olcott's Sri Lankan protégée Anagarika Dharmapala. Also present was Soyen Shaku, a Japanese Zen abbot, accompanied by Zenshiro Noguchi, his translator.

This was followed by the first public convert to Buddhism: Charles S. Strauss, a New York businessman. Shortly afterwards appeared the first American Buddhist magazine, *The Buddhist Ray*, followed by *The Light of Dharma*, from Jodo Shinshu missionaries.

Modern American Buddhism

D. T. Suzuki's books and essays were significant in spreading interest in Zen in the West. His work on translating the *Tao te Ching*, Asvaghosha's *The Awakening of Faith in the Mahayana* and *Introduction to Zen Buddhism* with a foreword by J. Carl Jung were key events in establishing Buddhism as a practice that was to be taken seriously by the educated elite.

Meanwhile, ethnic Buddhists represented by Jodo Shinshu had organised themselves into the Buddhist Mission of North America (the BMNA). Sokie-an founded the First Zen Institute of America in New York in the 1930s.

On the West Coast, the Chinese community is largely catered for by Hsi Lai Temple in Hacienda Heights, built in 1988 and costing $10 million.

New Trends in the United States

Soka Gakkai International, an organisation based on the teachings of the Nichiren School of Mahayana Buddhism founded in Japan in 1930, has seen enormous number of converts. There is no meditation and a minimum of organisation. Their members chant the 'Nam Myoho Rengo Kyo' and sections of the Lotus Sutra.

Engaged Buddhism is a new development following the work of Thich Nhat Hanh, a Zen Buddhist monk from Vietnam who became a peace activist.

The Buddhist Peace Fellowship was founded in 1978 by Robert Aitken and others, including Gary Snyder and Jack Kornfeld.

Buddhist Festivals

The major events of the Buddha's life are celebrated: his birth; his enlightenment; his death; as well as memorial days for great teachers.

Wesak (or Buddha Day) is celebrated on the full-moon day in May in countries that have Theravada Buddhism. On this day the qualities of the Buddha are recalled and celebrated.

Parinirvana Day (or Nirvana Day) celebrates the life of the Buddha and gives people time for reflection. The Paranirvana Sutra is often read, and Buddhists celebrate by meditating and visiting Buddhist temples or monasteries.

In Japan the enlightenment of the Buddha is celebrated on 8 December and the birth of the Buddha on 8 April.

Losar

This is the Tibetan celebration of their New Year. It is celebrated in February, although the exact date in that month varies according to the lunar calendar.

Losar carries over onto three days. On the first day the celebrations are family centred. On the second and third days Tibetans visit friends and relatives and exchange gifts. They also visit monasteries and make offerings to them.

Various rituals are performed to drive away evil spirits, including symbolic purification by cleaning thoroughly and then whitewashing buildings and by people wearing new clothes and eating newly prepared food. Celebrations include feasts and dancing.

Kathina

This Theravada festival originated some 2,500 years ago and is held either in October or November, at the end of the Vassa, or monsoon period.

Buddhist monks would have spent the preceding three months in a place to shelter from the monsoon and to meditate and reflect.

The Kathina festival celebrates the fact that they are ready to move amongst the people once again and includes offerings of cloth, given to the monks.

It is the largest alms-giving ceremony of the year. Monks are presented with cloth on behalf of the whole community. The monks then spend the night preparing and cutting the cloth and sewing it to create a robe.

Customs

There are a number of different customs and practices that take place in different parts of the world.

Venerating the Buddha

This usually takes the form of meditating on the qualities of Buddha. Alternatively, honouring the Buddha or Buddha figure by making offerings to images of the Buddha or relics.

The Exchange of Gifts

Theravada Buddhists will often give gifts to Buddhist monks. This is widely encouraged as it is seen as a desirable thing to give gifts to one another, as well as to good causes.

It is the monk's responsibility to share the fruits of their Buddhist practice and understanding with the rest of the community. These are considered to be gifts to the community at large, through teaching and simply by providing a positive role model or example.

On the converse, it is therefore seen to be of benefit to the wider Buddhist community for them to give gifts to monks, in return. In addition to this, this also wins them merit.

Pilgrimage

There are four key locations which are directly associated with the Buddha's life and were certainly the focus of pilgrimages within the first two or three hundred years after the Buddha's death.

Since this time, wherever Buddhism has established itself, new centres of pilgrimage have developed to reflect particular customs and practices.

For a Buddhist, a pilgrimage is usually undertaken to fulfil a vow or to strengthen their spiritual discipline. For many Buddhists pilgrimages assist them in expressing their devotion, as well as trying to create a link or relationship with historical figures or places.

368

Theravada Ordination

There are usually three stages: the Anagarika (postulant), the Samanera (novice, Sramanerika for women) and the Bhikku or Bhikkuni (fully ordained monk or nun).

The Postulant stage will usually take eight vows, novices 10, probationary nuns 36– 42, fully ordained monks 227 and fully ordained nuns 311. These are taken directly from the Pali Vinaya. There are periods between each ordination stage. The Postulant period is usually the shortest. There is an interim period for women, known as the Siksamana, which was established to ensure they were not pregnant at the time of their ordination.

Rites of Passage

An individual, before joining a monastic Sangha, must complete two rites of passage. They must renounce their secular life and accept monasticism as a novice.

Precepts

These are a condensed form of Buddhist ethical practice.

They are taken as recommendations, not commandments.

It is the spirit of the precept that counts, not the text.

Buddhist Cuisine

There is no specific prohibition to eating meat but butchery is considered a profession that is not particularly conducive the spiritual life for the majority of people. Meat is said to inflame the passions and is avoided for that reason alone.

Most monasteries in southern Asian countries cook rice as a staple and include vegetables. Food is simple and nutritious. Considerable attention is paid to making the food palatable and enjoyable to eat.

The Thangka Painting

The Thangka painting was probably
created in the 16th century and depicts
the Adi Buddha, or Vajradhara, the
bearer of the adamantine sceptre.

It is a visual expression of the totality of
Buddhist teachings, allowing abstract concepts
to be made accessible through the image.

The image has symbols of wisdom and
compassion and this demonstrates the
totality of enlightenment.

Buddhism Today

'Since we are never born, how can we
cease to be? This is what the Heart Sutra
reveals to us. When we have a tangible
experience of non-birth and non-death,
we know ourselves beyond duality.'

Thich Nhat Hanh

'Are you the Messiah?' asked the student.

'No,' answered Buddha.

'Then are you a healer?'

'No,' Buddha replied.

'Then are you a teacher?' the student persisted.

'No, I am not a teacher.'

'Then what are you?' asked the exasperated student.

'I am awake,' Buddha replied.

Alan Cohen, Are you the Buddha

'People often confuse meditation with prayer, devotion, or vision. They are not the same. Meditation as a practice does not address itself to a deity or present itself as an opportunity for revelation.'

Gary Schnyder, The Buddhist Review

Resources

Picture Credits

All illustrations created by Lucy Robins, using images courtesy of Foundry Arts and the following picture sources:

Art Archive: 322, 345

Christie's Images: 93 (Duck and lotus box, © CKS Christie's Images Ltd); 94–95 (Buddha Shakyamuni, © Christie's Images Ltd); 119 (Buddhist Trinity, © Christie's Images Ltd); 137 (Vajrakila Mandala, © Christie's Images Ltd); 210–11 (Elephant, © Christie's Images Ltd); 235 (Virupaksa, © Christie's Images Ltd); 250 (Chakrasamvara, © Christie's Images Ltd); 261 (Milarepa, © Christie's Images Ltd); 379 (Dancing Hevajra, © Christie's Images Ltd)

Impact: 146, 282–83,

Istock: 14, 16–21, 23, 24, 26–28, 32–36, 38, 40–43, 46, 49, 50, 53, 55, 56, 58, 60–64, 66–67, 69–91, 98–105, 107, 109, 111–17, 120–22, 124–25, 126, 128–32, 134–35, 141–43, 145, 148–49, 150, 152–58, 160–66, 168–77, 180–82, 184, 186–87, 189–191, 193–97, 201–02, 204, 206–09, 212, 214–17, 219, 220–23, 225–26, 230–32, 236–47, 249, 252–54, 256–57, 259, 263, 264–68, 270–73, 276–81, 284, 286–87, 289–306, 309–15, 317–21, 330–31, 333–44, 346–50, 352–59, 361–64, 366–76, 381

Books

Barrett, T. H. *Zen – The Reason of Unreason*, HarperCollins, 1993 (The Little Wisdom Library)
Batchelor, Stephen *Buddhism Without Beliefs: A Contemporary Guide to Awakening*, Bloomsbury, 1998
Bodian, Stephan *Meditation for Dummies*, Wiley Publishing Inc., 1999
Brazier, Caroline *A Buddhist Psychology*, Constable and Robinson, 2003
Durden, Jo *The Essence of Buddhism*, Eagle Editions, 2004
Gach, Gary *The Complete Idiot's Guide to Understanding Buddhism*, Alpha Books, 2005
Goldstein, Joseph and Salzberg, Sharon *Insight Meditation Kit: A Step-by-step Course on How to Meditate*, Sounds True Audio, 1999
Gyatso, Geshe Kelsang *Transform Your Life: A Blissful Journey*, Tharpa Publications, 2001
Hagen, Steve *Buddhism Plain and Simple*, Arkana, 1999
Hendy, Jenny *Zen In Your Garden*, Godsfield Press, 2001
His Holiness the Dalai Lama *The Little Book of Buddhism*, Rider & Co., 2000
Jarmey, Chris *Book of Meditation*, Element Books/HarperCollins, 2001
Kyabgon, Traleg *The Essence of Buddhism: An Introduction to Its Philosophy and Practice*, Shambhala Publications Inc., 2001
Landaw, Jonathan *Buddhism for Dummies*, Hungry Minds Inc., 2003

Index